Praise for Total Immersion *from world-class competitors to weekend athletes*

"As new thirty-something triathletes with poor swim skills, we're singing the praises of *Total Immersion*. After two months of practice, our strength and comfort in the water is so vastly improved that it is mind-boggling. *Total Immersion* methods are innovative and apply to any skill set. We recommend TI for anyone who needs to improve his or her swim skills, and particularly novice swimmers."

   —Kevin Hirsch and Amy Barnhart

"*Total Immersion* is a wonderful contribution to swimming. I am so impressed I made it required reading for my swim school teachers and swim team coaches."

   —Forbes Carlile, M.B.E., M.Sc., Australian Olympic Coach
    1956 to 1992; Director, Carlile Swimming Organization
    (Australia's leading swim school)

"*Total Immersion* is the perfect way to teach and coach swimming. The relaxed and effortless improvements made by my swimmers are so impressive. Every time a swimmer finds his or her natural position in the water, he or she begins to move through it in such an efficient manner."

   —Coach Larry Blomberg, Deerfield Beach, Fla.

"The *Total Immersion* method makes such sense. Now I watch other swimmers beating themselves up while I'm gliding and skating and, better yet, enjoying my workout. It is as if I have a secret. Yes, my laps are happy laps."

   —Barb Lloyd

"Inspiring . . . With the help of *Total Immersion,* I swam 50 yards five seconds faster than I ever had before, taking seven fewer strokes than my previous best. For the first time in my life I feel like a swimmer."

   —Keith Weaver

"After swimming the *Total Immersion* way, I will never go back to the old way of swimming again."
—Thom Peters

"After swimming poorly for twelve years, two months with *Total Immersion* have been awesome."
—Dan and Jackie Cipriani

"I have been so amazed that I can swim faster and have a better stroke. Words cannot fully express how happy I am for this book. Happy laps!"
—Marven T. Ayson

Total Immersion

The Revolutionary Way to Swim Better, Faster, and Easier

— REVISED AND UPDATED —

Terry Laughlin

with John Delves

A Fireside Book
Published by Simon & Schuster
New York   London   Toronto   Sydney

FIRESIDE
Rockefeller Center
1230 Avenue of the Americas
New York, NY 10020

This Fireside Edition 2004

FIRESIDE and colophon are registered
trademarks of Simon & Schuster, Inc.

For information regarding special discounts for bulk purchases,
please contact Simon & Schuster Special Sales at 1-800-456-6798
or business@simonandschuster.com

Manufactured in the United States of America

30

Library of Congress Cataloging-in-Publication Data
Laughlin, Terry.
    Total immersion : the revolutionary way to swim better, faster, and easier /
Terry Laughlin with John Delves.—Rev. and updated.
        p. cm.
    "A Fireside book."
    Includes bibliographical references and index.
    1. Swimming—Training.   I. Delves, John.   II. Title.
GV837.7.L38 2004
797.2'1—dc22   2004044977
ISBN -13: 978-0-7432-5343-7
ISBN -10:   0-7432-5343-4

I dedicate this book to three gentlemen from the world of swimming who enriched my life beyond measure:

To Coach Dick Krempecki, who coached me at St. John's University, who inspired me to want to be a swimming coach.

To Coach Bill Irwin, who coached me at Manhasset Swim Club, who inspired me to be a swimming coach who teaches.

To Coach Bill Boomer, who opened my eyes to a whole new way of teaching.

— Acknowledgments —

In 1995 when I wrote the original edition of this book, I benefited from the help of quite a few people. John Delves, who had collaborated with me on numerous articles since 1990, acted as my "surrogate reader" and helped shape my text to read well and clearly for non-swimmers and new swimmers. He was the best writing teacher a swimming coach could have. My brother Steve Laughlin produced all the line drawings found within. My original editor Becky Cabaza had great enthusiasm for swimming and the printed word. For the updated edition, Doris Cooper smoothly guided the project to completion, and Katie Myers seamlessly improved my prose.

Alice McHugh Laughlin, my wife and partner since 1974, has been selfless and unconditional in her love and support through the ups and downs of a life in swim coaching and kept me organized so I could devote myself to coaching, teaching, and writing about swimming. My daughters Fiona, Cari, and Betsy have selflessly shared their dad with swimmers around the world on countless weekends, and—I am delighted to say—have all now become trained as Total Immersion Teaching Professionals.

— Contents —

PART ONE: NEW MOVES
Teaching Yourself to Swim a Whole New Way

Chapter 1

Chapter 2

Chapter 3

Chapter 4
Tuning the Engine: Finding—and Using—

Chapter 5

Contents

PART THREE: SWIMMING FOR LIFE
Be Healthy, Be Strong, Be Happy—Here's How

Contents

Total Immersion

— Introduction —

Let me ask you three questions:

1. Does swimming make you feel *good*—both physically and in overall satisfaction?
2. Do you feel you know what it takes to get better—not guesswork, but *guaranteed?*
3. Are you progressing steadily—even if slowly—toward greater efficiency and understanding?

If you can't answer *yes* to all three questions, if you feel any discomfort, frustration, or confusion about swimming, if you've ever had an unsatisfying experience with swim instruction or coaching, it's not because there's anything wrong with you. The way you were taught—indeed, even the way you've been led to *think about* swimming—is to blame.

Virtually everyone—the tiny percentage of "natural" swimmers excepted—has had similar experiences. The problem is that while fish and aquatic mammals are ideally designed for moving through water efficiently, we're not. Virtually everyone's first swimming attempt is a near-death experience, with a real prospect of drowning if you're not successful. And it doesn't get much better after that: Despite the fact that swimming is an essential life skill, *it has never been taught correctly.* Traditional (i.e., Red Cross) instruction teaches you to *not drown* rather than to emulate what works so well for fish. If you continue reading, all that is about to change for you!

How Total Immersion Revolutionized Swimming

The first edition of this book was published in 1996. Within months, with neither fanfare nor advertising, it became the world's best-selling book on swimming. The reason? Everyone who read it began to swim better, and to enjoy swimming more, immediately. They finally understood what really matters in swimming. And they found themselves making steady progress for the first time ever. In the past six years, I've heard from thousands of readers, all expressing these sentiments: "Thanks for writing about swimming *in a way that makes sense* and for making swimming a truly pleasurable activity."

These messages have been enormously gratifying, as I had really hoped to provide a swimming-improvement method that anyone could understand and follow. Moreover, by practicing what I teach, I've reached a personal nirvana where *every lap I swim feels blissful*. Because I've never been a gifted athlete, I became convinced that the joy of swimming well is attainable by everyone, rather than a gift reserved for a talented few. My mission as a teacher has been to bring that gift to as many people as possible.

Enthusiasm for the TI approach—from all manner of swimmers, from novices to national champions (and coaches and teachers, too)—confirms that Total Immersion *works*! It doesn't matter if you're age three or forty-three or seventy-three—or whether you've never swum before or have set bushels of records. Total Immersion can turn anyone into a swimmer or make you a better swimmer than you are now.

In the past few years, TI has become a "movement." Virtually everyone who has been introduced to TI, after reading the book, attending a TI workshop, or even watching a TI swimmer glide back and forth in the local pool has recognized that, as the title promises, it's revolutionary. Dan Schaffer, of Brooklyn, New York, recently wrote me that after his first experiences of teaching TI, the unvarying enthusiasm of his students convinced him that "fifty years from now, if someone decided to write a definitive history of swimming, your book would be cited as the main influence for when swimming changed."

Total Immersion teaches swimming in a way that no one ever has before. We call the TI method *Fishlike Swimming,* and the way swimming is usually taught *Human Swimming.* Conventional teachers and coaches focus on pulling, kicking, muscling your way through the water and endless laps to condition you for the ordeal of more and more laps—activities that mainly reinforce all that is wasteful about Human Swimming. TI instructors teach you to be balanced, slippery, and fluent—and to devote your pool time to thoughtful practice that turns these efficient movements into rock-solid habits.

Here is how TI will change your swimming:

- **You'll learn to be Fishlike.** Rather than churning out endless laps of pulling and kicking, you'll learn to swim with the effortless grace of fish. You'll feel the difference from your very first lap of intelligent, purposeful TI practice.
- **You'll learn the *qualities* of beautiful swimming as well as the mechanics.** While your initial goal is probably to swim

faster, you'll quickly realize that it's far more important—and more satisfying—to swim with grace, flow, and economy. Speed will surely follow if you first master ease.

- **You'll achieve transformation along with fluid strokes.** TI, alone among all swimming-improvement programs, teaches swimming as a *practice*—in the same mindful spirit as yoga or tai chi. By swimming the TI way you'll sharpen the mind-body connection leading to heightened self-awareness and self-mastery, and greater physical *and* mental well-being.
- **You'll master swimming as an art.** TI emphasizes the same studied precision and refinement taught by martial-arts masters. You'll start with simple skills and movements, will progress by small, easily mastered steps, and will thrive on the attention to detail and the logical sequence of progressive skills.

Overnight your swimming will be transformed from "following the black line" into a "moving meditation" that *always* feels good and is as mentally engaging as it is physically pleasurable. That's important because if you swim for the sheer pleasure of it—rather than from a sense of obligation—you'll swim for life. And as we've found, even if your primary reason for swimming is to win races, the movements that *feel* the best are also those that help you *swim* your best.

What's New in This Edition?

The book *Total Immersion,* as originally published, has worked wonderfully for thousands of swimmers. Yet the process we use to teach Fishlike Swimming, as described in chapter 8, has been dramatically refined as the result of thousands of teaching experiences since 1996. By 2001, our instructional sequence had become easier for every student to learn and the progression from basic drills to advanced drills to whole-stroke swimming had also become far more seamless. Only two of the twelve steps described in the original chapter 8 remain in the fourteen steps of the updated sequence. Our new learning sequence was working so much better that I thought it essential to update this book.

Chapters 1 to 7 remain unchanged from before, as they still explain simply and clearly why swimming lap after lap has done little for you and why *slipping your body through the smallest possible "hole" in the water* has far more of an impact on your swimming than *how you use your hands to push water toward your feet.* Once you've read chapters 1 to 3, go ahead and dive right into Lessons 1 and 2 in chapter 8. These body-balancing-and-streamlining exercises are the foundation of everything to come. The skill drills in chapter 8 are so simple you could really start doing them without any preparation, but they'll mean more—and possibly work faster for you—if you understand *why* they work, how they'll feel when you get them right, and how you'll gradually integrate them into your regular swimming, which is covered in chapters 4 to 7.

Once you begin swimming in a new way, you should practice differently, and part 2 shows you how, explaining how and why "conditioning is something that happens to you while you're practicing good technique." You'll see that from now on, "mastering flow and eliminating struggle" always comes before "muscle power."

Fishlike Swimming is something people want to enjoy for a long time, and the advice in part 3 on strength training, weight loss, and injury prevention will help make that possible. So will the exciting possibilities for doing things you may never have tried—from swimming in open water to competing in Masters Swimming or a postal meet where you mail in your times.

The message is simple: Forget everything you've heard about swimming; the old way is difficult to follow, frustrating, and wastes your energy and time by concentrating on the wrong things. To become a good swimmer you need neither brawn nor youth, neither great athleticism nor impressive endurance. You need fluent movement and an intelligent, thoughtful approach to making Flow a habit. With this book as your guide, you'll have both.

PART ONE

New Moves:

Teaching Yourself to Swim a Whole New Way

Swimming Laps and Going Nowhere

It's no mystery why people have trouble swimming as fast or as far or as smoothly as they'd like: Most of them are doing it backward. "Don't worry if your form's not perfect," coaches and instructors have always assured us. "Just get those laps in. Eventually, you'll be fit enough to develop a smoother, stronger stroke." It really works the other way around, but that's not how it's been taught.

Until now. Let me tell you how I came to discover what good swimming is *really* all about, and what this means to anyone who would rather spend his or her time growing faster and smoother instead of just growing tired—and who wants to do it all as quickly as possible.

But first, a confession. I'm addicted to the sport of swimming. I leave my house at 5:30 most mornings to keep my daily swimming "appointment," I compete in meets and open-water events whenever I can, and last but not least, I earn my living teaching other adults how to become addicted too.

Hard to imagine it any other way because, in my opinion, swimming is more fun than anything else you can do with your clothes on. It feels great and, no matter how hard the workout, you're left so refreshed, so energized, that for the rest of the day no challenge seems too great.

Name one other workout that can do that. After running, I ache all day long and often into the next. Cycling is fun and is certainly fine exercise, but only as long as the sun's up and it's not cold or wet out. Weight training is excellent, but by the time I'm done, it's all I can do to carry my gym bag back to the car.

Swimming's different. I always feel better after my workout than I did before. That's what makes it so easy to leave a comfortable bed even before sunup on a frosty morning, or on a sultry summer predawn, to get to the pool on time.

Perhaps calling swimming "the ideal exercise" is a little strong, but it would be hard to find a better contender for the title. It makes your heart and lungs work more efficiently, enhances muscle strength and endurance, improves flexibility, and helps reduce stress. Yet swimming is easier on the joints than anything else that gets your heart rate up. Unless you count cross-country skiing, swimming uses more muscles than all other exercises. And it's the only one that can legitimately make you feel weightless and free.

Tired of the battle scars of other aerobic sports? Swimming is about as injury-free as they come. Gone are the bone-jarring shocks of land sports, so gone too are the joint and back injuries that plague so many joggers and cyclists. The water is also kinder to your muscles. Its massaging effect and the steady, even resistance it provides eliminate much of the postworkout muscle soreness so common in land sports.

Overheating is also nearly impossible in swimming. Water conducts heat from the body twenty times better than air does, so you can train at much higher intensities—in summer particularly—without the dehydration and potential heat exhaustion common "ashore."

And swimming is an equal opportunity sport. Even if your weight, a physical handicap, or an injury would normally keep you out of action on land, you can probably swim. In fact, many land athletes use swimming to regain strength and fitness after an injury, far sooner than they could by returning to their main sport.

Joints growing stiffer with time? One of the most important reasons for an adult to swim is to increase flexibility, because this sport promotes joint mobility better than any other aerobic exercise. And while swimming's no fountain of cardiological youth, a 1988 study by cardiologists and exercise physiologists at the University of Texas Health Science Center in Dallas showed that inactive adults improved their heart function significantly within just three months of beginning a swim-training program. Their hearts beat more slowly and powerfully and circulated blood more effectively. Regular swimmers have also been shown to have lower blood pressures, slower pulse rates, and much greater exercise tolerance than other people their age. On top of all this, the aerobic benefits of swimming one mile are equal to those of running four miles.

None of this mattered—since little of it was known anyway—when I swam in college. Swim training was simple then: You stepped up and took your medicine. Take enough of it as often as possible and you'd win the race you were training for. It was *supposed* to hurt, or you had no business calling yourself a competitive swimmer. And who could ask questions when your heart was always pounding and your muscles never stopped aching?

But the time for questions was coming, and it finally started during a thirty-plus-year coaching stint after college. At last, I could watch other swimmers from the pool deck as only a coach can. What an eye-opener! I finally realized that somehow, for some reason, a gifted few were able to swim extremely well without even breathing hard. It turned out to be no illusion. During some personal coaching, I was astounded to find they could, in fact, swim that well with comparatively little effort. And apparently it was that efficiency, not any unusual capacity for grueling work, that kept them consistently ahead of their competitors.

Was this an inbred gift or could it be taught, I wondered. Too soon to know for sure, but the signs were already there. Time after time, average swimmers would suddenly start improving when I stopped them from doing nothing but beating themselves up with hard training and started them on drills and exercises that let them use their existing power better.

Truth to tell, I enjoyed "cheating the system." By teaching my athletes to be more efficient than their rivals, I gave them an edge they could use to outperform swimmers who trained for many more hours—all of which saved me a lot of time on deck. Let's be honest: Even a dedicated swim coach doesn't relish countless hours watching people grind out endless laps. And as I became a "stroke teacher" more than a workout monitor, I no longer had to.

Then, in 1988, everything began to fall into place and the real secrets of successful swimming became more obvious. That was the fateful year I met Bill Boomer and subsequently left college coaching to work exclusively with adults. Boomer, whom I refer to so often in my workshops that some campers probably think they've met him, was swimming coach at the University of Rochester in upstate New York. Though relatively unknown in the wider world of American swimming, Boomer had a cult following among other college coaches in the region, coaches whose teams regularly faced his—and not often successfully. His ideas about swimming were considered radical, even revolutionary, and obviously worth listening to.

One memorable day, Boomer addressed a coaches' clinic I happened to be attending. Speaker after speaker had gone on and on about how they trained their swimmers by "building the engine and fuel tank," so to speak—throwing enough hard work at them that their bodies had no choice but to build endurance.

Then Boomer took the podium and dropped his bomb. He posed an obvious question, but one I'd never heard in two decades of attending such meetings: "How can we teach people to swim, at any given speed, *with less effort?*" His answer was just as disarming, and just as radical: "By reshaping the vessel." After all, swimmers had a lot in common with boats, and like a naval architect Boomer knew there were ways to improve the efficiency of their "hull designs."

Detroit had been doing it with cars since the price of fuel shot out of sight in the early 1970s, but no one until Boomer had thought of visualizing swimming the same way. Apparently he simply had the advantage of fresh eyes and an open mind, since he hadn't even been a swimmer himself, studying movement science in school and coaching soccer and track. So Boomer came to swimming minus the usual baggage of how things "ought" to be done and with a deep understanding of the way the human body moves. That enabled him to see things the rest of us had missed.

Boomer didn't have to tell me twice. I knew right away that he was on to something, and working exclusively with adults gave me the unique opportunity to test it, develop it, and refine it. My Total Immersion workshops began concentrating on something no other swim coach in America had ever done: teaching swimming *technique* instead of giving workouts. In a sense, I was becoming more like a golf or tennis pro than a workout planner.

And the adult swimmers I was already specializing in were the ideal athletes to develop this with. As my training program grew far more sophisticated than just "more laps, more laps" and essentially became a program of precise technique, I had to make advanced skills easy to practice for older swimmers, most of whom had little experience in the sport and little understanding of what really made them move in the pool. None of us would get anywhere unless I figured out a way to distill relatively complex and advanced ideas into a series of simple, logical practice exercises that anyone could do. And since I had to travel to pools all over the United States each week, teaching a new group of students every time in just a few short days, the program had to be easily understood, quickly absorbed, and simple to practice after I was gone.

That was thousands of swimmers ago. Over the last few years my students have also been my partners in a long-running laboratory, making clear which instructions were too hard to understand or produced negligible results, helping me refine the ones that showed the most promise, and always being part of the search for a better, simpler, more direct route to better swimming.

Along the way, I learned that the usual "swim-your-laps" advice was not only ineffective; it could actually be harmful. If your form is making swimming difficult for you and you practice that form over and over, "following the black line," it's going to become more than bad form. It will become a bad habit. A hard-to-break one too, when you finally decide to.

Today, there's no question that swimming cannot be thoroughly understood nor effectively taught unless it's seen for what it is: primarily a skill sport like golf, tennis, or even skiing, rather than a power or endurance sport like running or cycling. And harder yet for people to accept is the fact that your skill is far more powerfully influenced by how you position and move your torso, or core, than by what you do with your arms and legs. Fanciful theory? Not at all. As you'll see later in this book, the world's top swimming scientists have discovered this to be true as they studied how world record holders swim.

A beautifully efficient stroke and the effortless swimming it makes possible are not prizes reserved for the lucky few who got them as gifts of nature or spent most of their waking adolescent hours grooming them. They can be taught. Contrary to much of the swimming advice you still hear, great technique is not an asset that carries a staggering price.

Lou Fiorina, an exceptional teacher who has coached with me at Total Immersion workshops, knows that now. But he didn't always. Fiorina remembers that when he watched Rowdy Gaines and Tracy Caulkins, both legends of American swimming, putting on a demonstration at a children's clinic several years ago, he thought, They're so fluid and graceful moving up and down the pool. You must have to be amazingly gifted to swim like that. Some months later, he went to another clinic. This time Bill Boomer was teaching a group of average college swimmers, and Fiorina was astounded by what was going on. "As I watched, I could see their strokes begin to show a lot of the same grace and elegance [as those of Gaines and Caulkins], and I suddenly realized that this stuff was *teachable,* that ordinary swimmers could learn to swim like elite athletes, and they could learn it fairly quickly."

Today they are doing just that at Total Immersion Weekend Work-

Swimming Laps and Going Nowhere

shops, using the exact principles you'll learn in this book, principles that are easily mastered by swimmers of any age. I've seen athletes in their seventies and eighties use these principles to improve their swim times and their fitness, *and* get the best possible workout in the bargain—doubling the payback from their pool time. The techniques are captured in a set of simple-to-learn skill drills, sequenced into a self-taught system different from anything you'll find anyplace else. Even athletes proficient in other sports but inexperienced as swimmers have learned to swim with an amazing degree of efficiency and beauty. This program can make any swimmer his or her own best coach.

Every minute of Total Immersion pool time is devoted to building proper technique, not by grinding out more and harder laps but by concentrating on fewer, easier, and more purposeful laps—stopping time-wasting "workouts" and focusing on efficient and effective "practice." Today, most swimmers who come to a Total Immersion workshop have been swimming for months or even years without seeing any progress. I hope I don't sound like a carnival barker when I tell you that when they learn the Total Immersion method, they begin to feel better and see improvement in their swimming almost immediately. You can too.

Where do the workouts go? Oh, you'll eventually do some speed and stamina training, but in the beginning at least, your fitness is an automatic dividend of skill building. If you want to improve your tennis game, do you spend forty minutes running back and forth between the baselines, getting in shape to chase shots? Not likely. You improve your tennis game by practicing your stroke for forty or forty-five minutes and, as you improve your game, you build the fitness you need to play tennis. We do the same thing in the pool, which is why I always open Total Immersion workshops with what I hope is welcome news to time-starved swimmers: *"Here, fitness is something that happens to you while you practice good technique."*

That's not just good news, it's good science. We now know that while conditioning matters, it doesn't matter nearly as much as we've been told. In fact, the world's top researchers estimate that champion swimmers owe about 70 percent of their great performance to perfect stroke mechanics and only around 30 percent to their fitness—a statistic you'll meet again and again in this book as we develop your new Total Immersion coaching strategy. For the rest of us "nonchamps," stroke efficiency is even more crucial, controlling perhaps 90 percent of our performance. Think about it. A new swimmer who does a quarter mile in ten minutes might shave five or ten seconds by whipping himself into better shape. But he could lop off a healthy 50 to 55 seconds simply by learning how to move more efficiently through the water.

Make no mistake: A good, efficient swimming stroke is one of life's more complicated skills, far more difficult to perfect than the ideal golf swing or the picture-perfect tennis serve. You can't come close without some expert instruction. But good teachers for adults have been hard to find, teachers who don't drown you in such a baffling sea of detail on how to move your arm every inch of the way that you forget which arm you're moving in the first place.

Worse yet, your armstroke actually has a very limited impact on how fast you move through the water. Take a horribly inefficient one and make it nearly perfect, and you might eke out a 5 percent or 10 percent increase in speed. That's because water is 1,000 times denser than air and throws huge drag forces against anyone who doesn't know the tricks of becoming slippery. Learning to cut that drag by improving your body position could well give you a 20 percent to 30 percent speed boost in just a day or two. It happens all the time at Total Immersion weekend workshops.

That's why we teach swimming "from the inside out," just the way you'll learn it in this book. First, we show you how to get the body balanced, streamlined, and stabilized. Then, we get to work on your propulsion system—but only the parts that matter.

This way opens a world of new rewards. With your body working as it was meant to, swimming becomes a pleasure all by itself, not just an exercise or a sport to compete in. And when you concentrate on form, which is the key to this program, you will not only become fit and efficient, you'll also find yourself developing an inner focus, like students of yoga or tai chi.

Grace, speed, technical proficiency, fitness, *and* peace of mind. Wait a minute—is this a swimming book or a whole human potential movement? You'll find the answer in the following pages, so let's get started. It's swimming we're going to be talking about, and you've no time to be skeptical. You've got more important things to do.

Swim Better Without Getting Any Stronger? Yes!

I wasn't always smart about swimming. In fact, like most everyone who competed in college, I spent four years doing it all wrong—though nobody realized it was wrong back then. No pain, no gain, we were warned. So hour after wearying hour, we put up with the pain. Some of us got results; many of us got more than a little frustrated from time to time. The problem was simple: We were working very hard to accomplish the wrong things. And to this day, too many people are still putting themselves through that dead-end kind of drudgery.

It happened like this. Early in my freshman season—still a stranger to serious daily training—I was timed for my first 1650-yard swim, swimming's so-called metric mile. It took me about twenty-two minutes. The top swimmers in our conference were a good four minutes faster, so if I wanted to get anywhere in distance swimming, I had my work cut out for me. And the only way I could figure out to do that was to speed up my stroke—exactly what most improvement-minded swimmers think even today. Hands move faster, body goes faster. What could be simpler? Besides, nobody bothered to disagree.

So each afternoon, my practice strategy was as simple as it gets: move the arms as fast as I could for as long as I could. Makes you tired in a hurry, I quickly found out, but I figured that by doing it every day

I'd get used to it—you know, teach my body to laugh at fatigue. And there was a certain medieval logic to it anyway. After diving into this punishment for two hours and 240 laps every afternoon in practice, race day felt like a breeze. It was over in under twenty minutes and 66 laps. What a snap! Call it primitive sport psychology, but I hadn't a doubt in the world I was doing the right thing.

And sure enough, within two years I had achieved my goal: swimming 18 minutes, to score in the Eastern Collegiate Championships. Victory! As I dragged myself out of the pool after finishing, the timer in my lane exclaimed, "I've never seen anyone move their arms that fast for that long!"

"Thanks," I muttered.

Neither of us understood at the time that it was not a compliment.

But I eventually found out. Because even though at that point I'd been training seriously for only two years. I never swam any faster. I had wrung all the potential out of my strategy. There was noplace else to find more speed.

Though I didn't realize it at the time—still doggedly determined to find some way to work harder yet—I had crashed into the limits of the most basic rule that governs how you produce swimming speed: $V = SL \times SR$. Velocity (V) is a product of how far you travel on each stroke (stroke length or SL) multiplied by how fast you take each stroke (stroke rate or SR). As you begin to approach the upper limits of how quickly you can move your arms, you can usually speed them up even more only by decreasing your stroke length. So it's a zero-sum game. Increase one and decrease the other by the same amount and your product—velocity—doesn't budge. Worse yet, you're burning up much more energy to achieve nothing. During my final two years of hard work in college, I perfected that frustrating formula.

But all that was about to change. The summer after graduation, I took my first coaching job. Finally I could analyze swimming from a comfortable position on the deck, a vastly improved perspective to determine what makes people fast in the water over what I'd had as a swimmer, frothing up and down the pool in a haze of pain. And from day one, it struck me plain as day: The fastest swimmers made it look the easiest.

The eggbeaters churning busily were all in the slower lanes, struggling in the wake of people who seemed to glide almost casually up and down. Could I have actually looked like those ineffectual water choppers? No doubt. So I staked out my first mission as a coach: to save my swimmers from repeating my mistakes. Instead of simply driving them to work as hard as possible, I would try to figure out what allowed my best swimmers to make it look so easy, then teach it to everyone else.

I operated on that instinct for the next twelve years, and it worked. Then, in 1984, we began to find out why. In a study conducted at the U.S. Olympic Swimming Trials, Bill Boomer and some sports science colleagues from the University of Rochester filmed every length swum by every swimmer in twenty-six men's and women's events over six days, a total of more than seven hundred demonstrations by some of the world's best of how to swim as fast as a human can.

Over and over, what they found was that 80 percent of the time, *the fastest swimmers took the fewest strokes.* And it was no fluke. Four years later, a similar study by Penn State researchers at the 1988 Olympics produced the same result. The swiftest swimmers were always the most efficient.

Swim Better Without Getting Stronger

So how could anyone learn to swim better and faster? We now had the answer: Work longer, not faster, strokes. In my own practices today, three decades removed from the disappointments of my college days, that's why I care less about how many yards I total than about *how many yards I travel on each stroke.* And that's why I never judge myself just by the pace clock when I'm trying to swim faster. Instead, I also measure how many additional strokes I need to gain that speed. In other words, what's it costing me?

So goal one for anyone who wants to swim better and faster is a longer stroke. This can happen in two ways: (1) more push—using your hands and feet to *thrust* your body farther through the water by making each stroke as powerful as possible; and (2) less drag—shaping your body so it's more friction-free, allowing it to travel farther with the power each of your strokes is already producing.

Of course, in the water your instincts "know" just what to do. Pull harder, kick harder, spin your arms faster. All wrong, of course. That's how I squandered four years of college swimming. Too bad I didn't know then what twenty-five years of coaching has taught me about how the world's best swimmers actually produce *their* speed. Most of it comes from how well they shape and position their bodies to eliminate drag and become more "slippery"—relatively little from how they use their hands and arms to push the water around.

A freestyler sprinting at world-record pace puts out over a thousand watts of power to "streak" down the pool at a paltry 5 mph. Yet fish have been clocked at 68 mph—as fast as a cheetah can run—with amazingly little energy expenditure. A 100-ton blue whale, cruising at 20 mph, should require some 448 horsepower, according to the calculations of Georgia Tech physics professor Vincent Mallette, but in fact gets by with fewer than 70. A dolphin also uses only about one eighth the power that simple physics says it should.

The human being, land-adapted for millions of years, struggles awkwardly when trying to propel himself through a substance 1,000 times denser than air. Every movement is bought at an extravagant cost in energy. To double speed in the water requires eight times as much power output. To swim but 10 percent faster requires a 33 percent increase in power. In the water, drag is everything. Active streamlining—avoiding water's drag—is the marine mammal's secret. And that, by shaping and positioning the body sleekly, rather than trying to pull powerfully, is the easiest way for humans to become more fishlike. In fact, kinesiologists estimate at least 70 percent of your swimming performance is determined by how well you streamline your body and only 30 percent by how fit or powerful you are.

So now we can begin to make that swimming-speed formula, $V = SL \times SR$, work for us instead of against us. First, you have to learn how to position your body so it moves as far as it possibly can with each stroke (SL); then you have to get fit enough to take those strokes at a higher rate (SR). But not too high.

Virtually every swimmer I see already has all the SR they'll ever need; it's the SL they're lacking. They always make their most dramatic improvements when they give up a bit of their SR in order to gain a lot of SL. So I always counsel swimmers to work on their SL first. Besides, energy consumption increases as a cube of muscle movement speed, so stroking twice as fast burns eight times as much energy. Not a great return on your investment.

I spent four years of college swimming trying to maximize SR and ignoring SL. No wonder I hit a speed ceiling. SL goes up when you

Swim Better Without Getting Stronger

use your brain. SR can only improve when you work on brawn, so its improvements are short-term and certainly can't go on forever. If you not only want to swim well but expect to do it for a lifetime, just look at the balance sheet. Then tell me which part of the swimming-speed equation you'd rather work on:

➤ SL is skill-oriented. You get better by improving your body's position or profile.

➤ SL improvements depend on brain-power. You use your knowledge, body awareness, and concentration to maintain sleek, efficient positions in the water. That's nervous system—instead of aerobic system—training. The energy cost is minimal.

➤ SL can be improved at any age. There's no such thing as "too old," because it's skill-oriented, and our ability to learn or improve SL remains acute far into our seventies, allowing smart swimmers to gain speed well into middle age and beyond.

➤ SR is training-oriented. You have to work hard to build up your muscles and energy systems to make those limbs move fast.

➤ SR improvements depend on working your heart and lungs harder—*much* harder.

➤ SR is age-limited. Eventually, your muscles just won't move any faster. The fuel for a high SR is provided by your aerobic capacity—the total amount of oxygen your muscles can burn to produce energy—which usually peaks at about age forty. That means your ability to increase your SR peaks too.

➤ SL improvements are permanent. Skills, once learned, become permanently imprinted in our "muscle memory." Invest time and effort in improving your SL and you won't lose it when you take a break from training.

➤ SR improvements are temporary. They demand fitness and fitness is transient, as anyone who's had to quit working out for a couple of weeks can tell you. Stay away just a little too long and you're right back where you started, forced to do the work all over again to rebuild that capacity.

The best—and smartest—of the world's elite swimmers try to eke out further speed increases with the least effort by splitting the difference. If your stroke gets longer but the rate stays the same, you will swim faster. If your stroke rate goes up and you manage to keep the length the same, you will also swim faster. But if you increase both by just a little bit, you will swim *much* faster. They establish SL first, then try to gradually increase SR, giving up the least possible SL in return. It's a delicate trade-off and one that the most successful swimmers practice unrelentingly.

Let's go back to that little speed statistic I mentioned earlier, the one about 70 percent of your ability to improve your stroke length coming from eliminating more of the water's drag on your body. It's not only true, it's the key to how great swimmers make their remarkable speeds look so graceful and effortless. That's no illusion. Relatively speaking, they *are* effortless. And learning to glide as far as possible after each stroke is the single most powerful skill they know. So we clearly want to devote the majority of our time and effort to becoming better "eliminators" when we swim.

It's a two-part strategy. First, play the game below the average speed line on your velocity curve (see illustration). Though you probably don't realize it, your body doesn't move at a constant swimming speed. During every stroke cycle, you accelerate and decelerate like a driver gently pressing and releasing the gas pedal. As you begin your stroke, the position of your arm and shoulder offers little leverage or power. Pull farther under your body toward your hips, and your arm moves into a much more effective position, one where the powerful torso muscles begin to help out. Up goes your speed. Then, as you finish the stroke and slice your hand out of the water, you begin to lose speed again. And you'll continue losing it until your other hand starts the next cycle.

Most people strain to swim faster by pulling or kicking harder or turning their arms over faster. They're trying to push the top of that speed curve a little higher before it slopes back down on the other side. Very wasteful. But if they worked on another part of the curve instead, they'd get where they're going faster and with much less exertion.

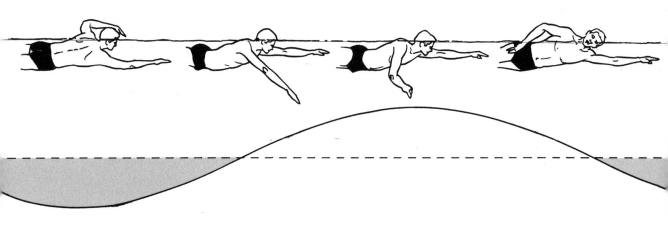

True swimming speed, of course, is not the top of the curve at all but the line that runs through the curve midway between the peaks and valleys—the average of your fastest and slowest progress during each stroke cycle. The amount of drag the water throws against your body is determined, in part, by how fast you're moving, and drag is much higher at the top of the velocity curve than at the bottom. So if you try to gain speed at the top of the curve, you bang up against a figurative brick wall. But there's far less resistance to speed improvement at the bottom, making it a smarter place to get faster.

That's why *what you do between strokes is actually more important than how you take the stroke.* Look at the illustration. Where is your body moving slowest, which is just where you can most easily add speed? Right. During the recovery. So keep your body long, balanced, and sleek during the recovery, and you'll boost performance far faster than anything you can do at the moment with your hand.

It's welcome—and extremely unexpected—news to people who all their lives have been told that pulling and kicking harder and faster is

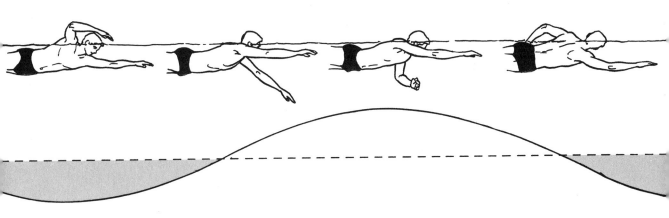

Swim Better Without Getting Stronger

the way to gain swimming speed. When I spring this fact on swimmers at my Total Immersion adult swim camps, they realize that what we'll be learning there, just as we'll learn in this book, is an assault on the conventional wisdom of swimming. It does nothing less than turn upside down and inside out the common understanding of what good swimming is all about. Great swimmers move so fast and take so few strokes not simply because they stroke powerfully but because their bodies keep slicing forward—quickly—for a long time after each one.

And it's an ability all of you can improve, whether you're headed for the Olympics or just for the Y. You may have a perfectly fine stroke and still take too many, because your body lurches too abruptly to a halt after each one. You have no choice but to keep those arms turning over because you don't conserve the momentum you do create.

You need to learn a few tricks that will make you more slippery. They come naturally to fish, but the rest of us can pick them up too, once we know what they are. By the end of the next chapter, you will.

The Slippery Swimmer

Resistance—it's just what you want in the weight room, but it gets in your way in other sports. If you've ever struggled to bicycle straight into a 30-mph headwind, you know why tapered helmets, Aerobars, even aerodynamic water bottles, were invented: to make you as compact and slippery as possible. The less surface area the air has to push on, the easier you move.

And in swimming you move through a medium that's 1,000 times denser than air! So while the need to become as streamlined as possible in swimming may be less evident because of the slower speeds you attain, it's actually more important. All efficient swimmers—which means nearly all the fast ones—seem to have a more instinctive sense of how to keep their bodies in the best position for slipping easily through the water, gliding as far as possible with the least possible effort.

I talked with Rick Sharp, Ph.D., the director of the International Center for Aquatic Research in Colorado Springs. He told me that his lab's research had turned up a surprising result, one that proved eye-opening to even some of the world's top swimming researchers. "We've discovered that the fastest swimmers generally produce less propulsive force than sub-elite swimmers," Sharp explained. "Obviously they're capable of producing more propulsive force, but they don't need it to go fast." In other words, they're faster not because of how powerfully they stroke but because of how *slippery* they make their bodies. For these elite swimmers, learning how to achieve this level of efficiency was a trial-and-error process, but the "secrets" of how anyone can do it have been around for . . . well, forever.

That surprises a lot of people who tell me they've finally come to one of my workshops because "I need to learn the new techniques. I started swimming back in the fifties and the strokes have all changed since then." So it comes as a nice surprise when I tell them that good swimming form is not like hemline lengths or tie widths—subject to today's fashion and tomorrow's obsolescence every time a new "discovery" comes along. There are principles of efficient swimming that can't go out of fashion because they're based on the permanent laws of physics, on how your body will always interact with the water.

What probably *seems* new to some people is that, remarkably, these principles have never really been explicitly taught until now, even though they were discovered long ago by naval architects who had to find ways to design the fastest and most easily driven ships of all time. These nautical scientists did all the work. Today, all we have to do is get into the pool and use what they found out, which, when applied to human rather than naval vessels, comes down to three cardinal rules for going faster:

1. Balance your body in the water.
2. Make your body longer.
3. Swim on your side.

They sound like contortions. But they work like a charm.

Better Balance: The Biggest Energy Saver of All

Whenever a swimmer comes to me complaining that she needs to develop a stronger kick, I recall what I learned my first day on in-line skates not long ago. Like thousands of other people, I took up "blading" because it looked like a really fun way to get an outdoor aerobic workout. It turned out to be no fun at all, at least not the first time.

After maybe fifteen minutes, I had to turn around and struggle home, confused. A dull ache in my lower back was bothering me so much I had to quit. That's odd, I thought. My legs are doing all the work.

I resolved to keep plugging away at this "tough" new workout, adding more distance to each session until I'd whipped those flabby back muscles—Rollerblading muscles, I presumed—into shape. But the next time I laced on my skates, I found out it wasn't weak muscles but poor form that caused my fatigue. Some skaters, I noticed, flowed along like syrup, their speed seeming to come from effortlessly swaying side to side. Others lurched along with choppy, labored thrusts. From a distance, I suddenly realized the difference was not back or leg muscle strength but weight shift. The good ones knew just when and how to transfer their weight from one foot to the other.

A smooth skater would lean all his weight on the left skate and then, *at just the right moment,* shift it all over to the right. Like all other lurching skaters, I hadn't caught on to this technique. My two-hundred-pound bulk would teeter out way too far beyond my center of gravity, and those weary back muscles would have to snatch me back before I fell. Eventually, of course, they would have grown strong enough for the job, but by then I'd merely have turned into a strong, bad skater instead of simply a bad one. Smarter to learn balance.

Many frustrated swimmers make the same mistake. They know their hips and legs are dragging along far below the surface, and if they're lucky they also understand it's not only the most common stroke flaw but the most serious as well: It saps their energy faster than anything else can. So they grab a kickboard and grimly start churning out the endless laps they hope will strengthen their "problem" legs.

Only their legs aren't the problem.

That's because a poor kick isn't what's keeping them from swimming better. It's poor balance, just as I found that day on my blades. But in the pool it can be corrected practically on the spot. And when it is, these swimmers happily discover that a "weak kick" is no longer a problem. In fact, properly balanced, they hardly have to kick at all!

But proper balance in the water is not a gift of nature. It's something we earn through practice. The human body, you see, simply wasn't designed to float efficiently in the water. Evolutionarily speaking, we're put together to function well on land, where our long legs and low center of gravity are perfect for stability and mobility. Above the waist, we're mostly volume; the lungs, after all, are just big bellows. That means we're most buoyant between the armpits, rocklike lower down. It's only natural that our longer, heavier end wants to sink.

Churning your legs hard to compensate for the way nature put you together will wear you out. Worse, it's useless against the imbalance that's slowing you down. And it's the surest path to a poor triathlon, by the way, where the last thing you want coming out of the water—facing a bike ride and a run after that—is pooped leg muscles.

What you really need is a better way of getting those hips up where they belong.

And there is one. I call it "pressing your buoy." Here's how it works.

What happens if you push a beach ball into the water? Right. The water pushes it right back out. You have one place on your body that's buoyant like that—the space between your armpits. Call it your buoy.

Press your buoy into the water and the water will press back. But *keep* pressure on that buoy and you force the water to push your hips up instead. Just what you want. Simply letting water pressure ease them to the surface takes far less energy than trying to prop them up by churning away with your legs.

And you can help yourself by using the weight of your head like a counterweight. Remember, your body in water is like an unbalanced seesaw, its fulcrum somewhere between your waist and your breastbone. The longer, heavier end wants to sink. But use the weight at the opposite end and it levels off nicely. You do that by acting as though a steel rod ran from your waist through the top of your head. Keep that "connection" intact and you help your hips pop to the surface. Break the connection—lifting your head to breathe instead of turning it with your body roll, for example—and gravity will drag your hips and legs right back down again.

Later on, in chapter 8, you're going to learn the simple pressing-your-buoy drill that makes all this automatic. You'll also start "swimming downhill," leaning on your chest as you go. With just a little practice, you'll discover that by pressing your buoy as you swim, you can make the water support more of your lower body's weight. Your suddenly lighter hips and legs will be effortlessly skimming the surface just where they belong. You'll actually feel as if you're swimming downhill.

The illustration below illustrates the difference between what your body looks like when it sinks unevenly, hips and legs dragging, and what happens when you balance evenly by pressing your buoy.

I don't promise it will come easily for everyone. The less buoyant among us (usually those uncommonly lean triathletes and runners) find it a little tougher to get their hips all the way up. If you're among them, don't worry if your body rests an inch or two below the surface. You are not trying to float like a cork. You are trying to get your upper and lower body lined up nearly horizontal to the surface, with your hips and legs as close to it as possible. Do that and you'll cut drag enormously. Reduce drag and watch what happens to your speed.

The most prominent benefit most swimmers will feel from learning balance isn't necessarily a stunning increase in speed. They'll be more likely to just feel more relaxed in the water. Once they realize that

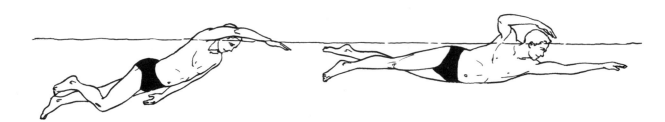

pressing the buoy causes the water to support more of their body weight, swimming becomes much less laborious. And a relaxed swimmer can do surprising things. One of my students, fifty-two-year-old Don Walsh from New Jersey, became so adept at swimming relaxed that after completing the Swim Around Manhattan in nine hours, he related, "I felt good the whole way and was never tired during the entire swim."

Longer Boats Are Faster. Longer Bodies Are Too.

When I was still pretty green at the coaching business, I was lucky enough to have two very gifted swimmers on my team and smart enough to realize I could learn more from them than they could from me. The first thing I noticed was that no matter how fast they swam, they made it look relatively effortless. That didn't come as such a surprise—I'd observed this in accomplished swimmers before— but why did they also somehow look *taller* in the water than everyone else?

The best swimmers, I've noticed over the years, always do. And it has little to do with their actual height. A skilled swimmer who is only 5'10" looks taller in the water than an unpolished swimmer who is 6'2", and it's no illusion. Better swimmers do "swim taller"—something anyone can learn—and because they do, they go faster. It's one of the fundamental principles naval architects have been using for over a century to design fast ships.

In the 1830s, a fever broke out among clipper ship owners to shatter the record for the fastest ocean crossings. The boats had only sails for power and couldn't simply install bigger engines, so more speed had to come from better hull design. W. Froude, a naval architect in England, tested various vessel shapes in a tank to learn which would produce the fastest design. His key discovery was that, all other things being equal, a vessel's drag decreases as its length at the waterline increases. Translation: Longer boats go faster—and easier. To this day, his calculations, known as Froude numbers, are used to predict the potential speed of various vessel designs.

What applies to clipper ships applies to you. In the vernacular of naval architecture, your body—along with racing yachts, rowing shells, or canoes—is a "surface-penetrating moving body" subject to many of the same laws. If a longer vessel can go faster, a taller swimmer can too. And taller swimmers do. In the 100-meter freestyle, swimming's premier sprint event, the fastest men in the world average about 6'6".

There are ways you can swim tall too, regardless of your height. And they are important to learn because they put mathematics powerfully in your favor. Take a hypothetical six-footer who swims the mile in 25 minutes. Feed him some growth hormone so he sprouts up to nine feet. He doesn't train any longer or harder, he doesn't get any stronger or fitter, he doesn't change his stroke in any way. He just gets taller. But his improved Froude number predicts that he can probably do the mile in 18 minutes!

Fine. But what if you're "only" 6'0" and at thirty-something quite likely to stay there? Well, as far as the water is concerned you can still grow, stretching your six feet to nearly nine feet from fingertips to toes by simply extending your arm overhead. And if you can stay in that extended—taller—position for more of each stroke cycle, you improve your own Froude number enough to go much faster on the same amount of energy.

Here's a simple experiment to prove it. Under water, push off the pool wall as hard as you can with your arms at your sides (the six-foot position) and glide as far as possible until you surface. Then do it again with your arms straight and streamlined overhead (the nine-foot position). See how much farther you go?

That's also the secret for swimming taller, what my mentor, Bill Boomer, calls front-quadrant swimming, or FQS. In the illustration below, consider the waterline as the x-axis and an imaginary vertical line through the shoulder as the y-axis. The two lines divide the swimming space into quadrants, the front quadrant being the one in front of the shoulder and under the water.

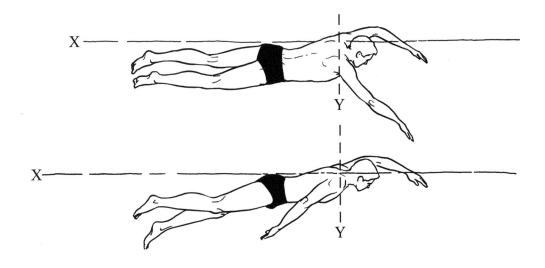

FQS swimming means always keeping one or the other of your hands in that front quadrant. (At the beginning of each stroke, of course, both hands are there.) It's really just another way of saying "swimming tall," of lengthening your body line and making you taller than you really are. Leave your right hand out in front while the left is stroking, then begin stroking the right just as the left returns to the front quadrant, and so on. One hand doesn't start until the other one's nearly back. Leaving each in place just a split second extra can make a big difference in your Froude number.

Common sense? Well, actually not so common. Why else would almost all the swimmers in my weekend workshops show up the first day as rear-quadrant swimmers? Why else would I have worked so hard when I was in college at being a rear-quadrant swimmer? Because it's easy to fall into the trap: "I move my body by pulling my hands back, right? To get it going faster, then, I just move my hands back faster, right? Gliding along with hands stretched in front? All that will do is slow me down!"

So my college swim strategy was like a bathtub windup toy: Dig in and pull back as soon as my hands touched the water. Unfortunately, it guaranteed that I would spend precious little time with either hand out in front of my head. I swam short, and it showed. I took 24 to 25 strokes per length, compared to the 14 or 15 I now use in my early fifties. Stroking fast was making it harder to *swim* fast.

Some people, as I was, are rear-quadrant swimmers by intent. But others can't help it—as soon as their hands enter the front quadrant, they're driven down and back. Their arms are "heavy" because of the weight they're supporting, weight that would be distributed elsewhere if their balance were better. Face it: You just can't be an FQS swimmer

New Moves

unless you're also a well-balanced swimmer. But whether or not your rear-quadrant tendencies are intentional, FQS is something no one does naturally. You have to know it matters, then consciously work on making it a habit, confident that you're taking another important step to becoming a faster and more efficient swimmer.

Done right, FQS is nothing less than a revolutionary way of thinking about what your hands do for you when you swim. Suddenly, you understand they contribute far more to your speed when used as body line extenders than when used to push water back. Once you've discovered that, you can use them more effectively to make you taller in a couple of ways.

First, use your hand to lengthen your body line before using it to stroke. This should be a true reaching action, like stretching up to a high shelf for something just out of your grasp. It should be as easy as extending your hand all the way forward first—not down—when it goes into the water. But for some people, it's not that easy. As soon as their hand hits the water, years of bad habits take hold and the arm automatically heads right for the bottom. It does, that is, until I ask them to pretend they're reaching for the wall as they would on the last stroke of each lap. As far as the muscles are concerned, that's different—now the arm goes out nice and straight and long. And the body glides along more easily behind.

Don't rush the process. Leave your hand extended before starting to pull back. Don't be in a hurry to start stroking. Chant silently, if it helps: "Enter, e-x-t-e-n-d, pause, and pull." Just let your hand keep gliding forward out there, reaching as long as possible before you begin stroking.

Second, make your arms better body line extenders by taking a load off them—literally—so they feel weightless. If you're pressing your buoy as I told you to, and if you're keeping your head's weight supported by the water and in line with your torso, you're already there. But if you are there, you're in the happy minority of the already balanced. If not, you'll want to work on a weightless arm using the specific drills in chapter 8, before trying to actually swim with one.

When you do, you'll find that the weight of those heavy arms and hands usually comes from one of two places:

1. You haven't put all your weight on your buoy, so some of it has gone back to your hips and legs, and they're sinking. To compensate, you're driving your hand and arm quickly down and out of the front quadrant. You're becoming shorter.
2. You're lifting your head—even the littlest bit—as you breathe. That shifts more weight to your hand, which has to support it. Down it goes too fast, over and over again, every time you breathe.

I promise it will take you a fraction of the time to learn that it took me. Swimming is not only my livelihood but my love, and I've been working on my stroke efficiency for years. But I was looking for speed in all the wrong places, minutely examining every movement of the hand through every centimeter of the stroke, and feeling lucky to shave maybe one stroke from my average every two years. Then I hit on the weightless arm and lopped off two strokes in just a matter of weeks. Then another after that. Believe me, when a professional coach's count per 25 yards tumbles from 16 to 13 strokes after almost thirty years of trying, he practically wants to tattoo instructions for the technique onto anyone who'll stand still. I'm *that* convinced.

So is coach Jacki Hirsty. Hirsty, a Masters swimming world record holder in the women's 35 to 39 age group, had been coaching with me on and off for five years. But it wasn't until we taught a Total Immersion workshop together in Boston that she heard about the weightless arm, a technique I'd finally polished up enough to share with students. The day after the workshop she tried it herself. She cruised through a set of 400-yard repeats faster than she had in several years, and on top of that her stroke count was actually lower.

Don't Swim Flat; Swim on Your Side

There's still another lesson swimmers can learn from boat designers: how to make their bodies fly like racing yachts instead of plowing along like scows. What are the fastest sailboats you can think of? Maybe the America's Cup contenders? With only the wind for power, they go like, well . . . like the wind. What's the slowest *powered* boat you can think of? It has to be the cargo barge. Load it up with as much horsepower as you want and it will still crawl. Well, we all have the choice of swimming like barges or America's Cup yachts.

One of the most enduring myths about our sport is that the correct position for swimming freestyle is lying on your stomach, turning your head to the side when you need a breath. Red Cross–trained instructors have taught millions to swim that way. And the few the Red Cross missed automatically swim that way too, because they just feel more comfortable and secure flat on their stomachs.

The Slippery Swimmer

But it's wrong. You don't swim freestyle on your stomach if you want to be any good (and by the way, you don't swim backstroke on your back either). The fastest, most efficient swimmers in the world cut the water on their sides, rolling from one side to the other with each stroke and staying on each side for as much of each stroke cycle as they can. The advantage is simple to understand: You slip through the water more easily that way than on your stomach.

Let's go back to naval jargon for a moment. You'll recall that your body—along with yachts and barges—is a surface-penetrating moving body, and that all of those are subject to the same physical laws because they all slice the surface as they go. (Submarines, torpedoes, and fish—as well as butterfly and breaststroke swimmers—hang out below the surface and are subject to slightly different hydrodynamics.) One of those laws is that drag or resistance goes up by the *square* of the distance the water travels to get out of your way. Twice as far equals four times as hard. So would you rather swim like a barge, pushing water in front of you, or like a yacht with the fluid slipping easily around you? Dumb question.

And you've actually understood this principle since you were a little kid, holding your arm out the window of the car. When you held it straight up, palm flat against the airflow like the traffic policeman's stop signal, the wind pushed it hard. Then, you bent your elbow so the palm faced down, fingertips pointing forward. Wow. Hardly any pressure.

Same thing applies to your (surface-penetrating) body in water. As you swim, water goes mostly around you to get out of the way. Very little slips underneath. On your stomach, you're like a barge with its "broad shoulders" forcing the water to move so far that it's constantly

New Moves

pushing along a huge volume of water in front. Yachts, on the other hand, even if they're broad in the beam, are knifelike up front, so it's easy for the water to go around, as shown in the illustration below. When you swim like a yacht, cutting water on your side, drag may be half as much as when you swim like a barge.

I know. You can't stay on your side forever. But you can roll from one side to the other as you stroke. The most efficient way to swim freestyle is to roll rhythmically until your shoulders and hips are a bit less than perpendicular to the water and to try to spend just a bit more time on your side in each stroke cycle.

Rolling also helps make your body a little longer. Prove it to yourself this way: Stand facing the wall closely, one arm straight overhead, palm flat against the surface. Leave your hand where it is, and turn your body to the side, then back again several times. Notice how your

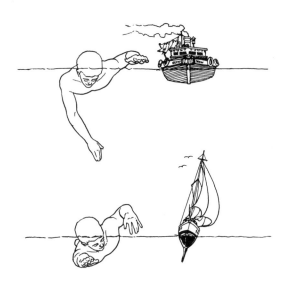

The Slippery Swimmer

hand slides up as you turn, and down as you turn back, making you "taller" each time you turn sideways and "shorter" as you turn back to face the wall? Same thing when you roll to your side: You swim taller.

Given all these advantages, you obviously want to roll on every stroke, ending up as close to a side-lying position as possible at the end of each one. The smartest thing you can do then is stay right where you are—on your side—as you return your arm to where it will reenter the water. As a consequence, you glide in the fast-moving side-lying position the whole time you're not stroking. And you glide farther and faster because you're not pushing all that water in front of you.

Done this way, freestyle becomes graceful, powerful, a feat of intelligent body engineering instead of a tiring exercise in plowing through the water. It becomes a series of long glides linked by quick rolls as you stroke and change sides. Each time, your body has a working side—the one you're pulling with—and a sliding side—the one that's making your body longer so the pull delivers all the speed and distance it can. The longer you stay on your side in each stroke cycle, the farther and faster your body will travel. Swimming also becomes much more restful and a lot less work. It even looks easier.

And that may drive some people crazy. While traveling to one of my workshops not long ago I was a guest at a Masters group's workout. After a single set, one of the swimmers in my lane came over to me and, with just a bit of an edge in his voice, said, "I can't figure out how you're keeping up with us. You don't look like you're *doing* anything." Well, compared to everyone else, I wasn't. They were churning their arms steadily, splashing mightily, and "getting the work done." I was like a sailboat, quietly gliding and resting on my side between strokes—and staying right up with them. Without roll and glide, they had no choice but nonstop arm turnover if they didn't want to stop dead in the water between strokes. Of course, my swimming didn't look like a lot of work. Compared to theirs, it wasn't. It may even have looked like cheating.

So why doesn't everyone swim this way? Are they gluttons for punishment? No. But even if most swim instructors didn't actually *discourage* people from something as valuable as rolling—which they do—you'd still see more "flat" swimming than anything else because that's how we feel more comfortable. Rolling to the side makes us feel unsteady, tippy, out of control. So we barely tip to one side or the other, and we certainly don't stay there a nanosecond longer than we have to. Facedown just seems right.

It's that old bogeyman, bad balance, and if learning to do it flat on your stomach took some practice, wait until you have to balance on your side. It's not natural, it's not instinctive, and it's difficult to learn without concentrated, conscious effort. But until you have it, you're going to avoid rolling and you'll settle for being a barge. And you don't have to settle, not when the skill drills in chapter 8 give you a step-by-step approach to ultimately feeling as slick as a racing yacht.

When I first said that streamlining your body probably accounts for about 70 percent of your potential swimming improvement, I expected those raised eyebrows. I always get them in my swim clinics too—until we jump into the pool and start shedding resistance-causing bad habits left and right. "I've never seen the bottom slide by so fast," someone will say, or someone else will report that they've just cut six strokes from their normal count for 25 yards. The drills we use are the same ones you'll find in chapter 8. Your results should be just as exciting.

But even I have to admit one thing: You can't glide if something didn't push you along in the first place. That's called propulsion, and just because I think it's overrated doesn't mean it can't be dramatically improved. First, though, you must forget the idea you probably have of needing powerful shoulders to drag the rest of your body down the pool. Then I'll tell you what *really* does the job, and how you can make it happen more powerfully.

Tuning the Engine: Finding—and Using— Your Swimming Power

4

"If your body were a motorboat, your engine would be in your hips. Your hands are actually nothing more than the tips of the propeller blades."

I learned that from my mentor Bill Boomer, and at first it sounded backward to me too. After all, I'd directed countless swimmers to spend hours in the weight room building powerful arms and shoulders. And now a coaching maverick was trying to tell me I'd had it all wrong? That they're not what moved me through the water in the first place? That I'd essentially been misleading my swimmers?

Well, yes, that's almost *exactly* what he was saying. When I paused to think about it, I realized that what he was saying made perfect sense even though, at the time, virtually no one else saw it that way. "Swimming is the rhythmic application of power" was another Boomer aphorism, an innocent but actually quite seditious statement, since it meant that rhythm (which swimmers seldom worked on), not power (which they worked on all the time), is what's actually at the heart of creating propulsion in brilliant swimming. Good body rhythms give you the power that the arms and shoulders simply deliver. And rhythm movements *must* originate in the body's center or core, not at the extremities (the arms and legs)—just the opposite of how swimmers have always tried to do it.

Boomer had seen to the heart of swimming propulsion, understanding the underlying physics of swimming while the rest of us were still just slapping the water. Propulsion—how we produce the force that actually moves us through the water—did not work the way we all thought it worked, Boomer told us. But few were open-minded enough to listen at the time.

You may be wondering, freshly convinced from the previous chapter on streamlining, whether your shape and balance might be all that really matters. But stop and think: Even though 70 percent of your potential speed improvements will indeed come from learning to slip through the water more easily using the techniques in chapter 3, that still leaves another 30 percent you can tap. And that 30 percent comes from learning a more economical and effective style of creating propulsion.

It's the second half of what I call the eliminate/create process: First eliminate drag, then create more power. That's exactly how you should work on it too. Start by understanding what it feels like to be in harmonious balance in the water, then shape your body so it evades frontal water pressure well, then learn to apply rhythmically powerful movement. We're now about to start installing the engine on your seaworthy vessel.

Not only does this put first things first, it saves the easier work for last. For while reducing drag is certainly not complicated, improving propulsion is simpler yet. If you've ever despaired of mastering all the seeming rocket science of "S-strokes," hand shape, and pitch or vortex patterns recounted in other swim books, we're about to make it much simpler and more lucid.

Better yet, the whole propulsion process follows from the techniques you've already learned to reduce drag. You're still swimming "inside out," first generating power by rolling your body from side to side and only then using your hands to deliver that power to the water. Once you master "eliminating," you're already doing most of what you need to do for "creating." So it's not a new course, just the second semester of the one you've already grown familiar with.

Get Hip to Your Swimming Power

I'll start off by telling you something that, at first glance, may make little sense: Your arms are not that important. Well, not the way you may think. Power in most sports—swimming included—originates much lower down in your body. In most cases, the arms are just the "delivery system."

Picture the smooth arc of a Tiger Woods drive off the tee. Or the explosive serve of a Serena Williams. Or the powerful *crack!* as Barry Bonds drives yet another one out of the park. Then think of the power it takes to slam a ball over 300 yards, or blast one over the net at 130 mph, or send it arcing 450 feet or more into the stands. What arms, eh?

Well . . . no. Arm swing may be what is most visible to us, but it's not what's doing the work. Arm swing is actually the last—and least powerful—of a linked series of actions, each of which takes its momentum from the one before. As the pitcher releases the ball, the batter's first action is to cock his arms and shoulders away from the ball (a so-called plyometric contraction like winding up a spring, storing energy that will later be released in the opposite direction). Then it all begins to unwind. He starts by stepping toward the pitcher as his hips take up the rotation and in turn power the torso around, which drives the shoulders toward the pitch. The shoulders pull the upper arms through, adding speed. The upper arms pull the forearms, and only after the forearms have gotten up to speed do the wrists snap, completing a crack-the-whip chain that finally drives the ball. Huge forces are generated by a combination of powerful muscles—mostly in the butt and torso—moving a maximum amount of mass with perfect timing.

So why do the same people who would go to their hips for their power if they were standing at home plate or on the tee think they ought to swim by spinning their arms like a windmill? A powerful stroke, like the one that results in a home run, should be driven by rhythmic rotation of the body starting, as does the batter's, at the hips. Remember the last technique we covered in chapter 3, the drag-diminishing body roll? Well, the same roll that lets water slip around you also conveniently produces virtually all of your stroking power. Yes, it's all in the hips, and you've already begun to direct them into purposeful rotation. When you do this, you're using the body's most powerful muscles, the gluteals (the butt muscles), to move your center of mass from side to side. And powerful muscles moving a large mass generate impressive force.

The arm and shoulder muscles don't really amount to much by comparison, so why struggle to use them as your engine? You wouldn't try to move your car with your windshield-wiper motor, would you?

Those arm and shoulder muscles are, however, superb stabilizers, and the way to take advantage of that is to use them to hold on to the water.

If nothing else, muscles that hold on don't get hurt like muscles that are trying to act like workhorses. Think of your arms and shoulders as the engine, and invariably you'll push them too hard. The best you can hope for is wearing yourself out too soon, and you will. Your arms quickly lose their punch because they're doing way too much, while the true workhorse muscles lower down are loafing along. Worse, you could be heading for an injury. Mother Nature really wanted your shoulder muscles to simply hold together and stabilize the joint, setting your arm in a maximum-leverage position where it can better hold the water against the powerful forces developed by your body roll. She never envisioned them driving your arms through the water by the hour, like a Mississippi River sternwheeler. So make this joint do most of the work moving you down the pool, and sooner or later Mother Nature is going to send you a big error message.

Tap the power in your real power source, however, and watch what happens. Where did all this fitness, this feeling you could go on forever, this freedom from fatigue, suddenly come from? Even the previously exhausting little trick of trying to accelerate your hand during the second half of each stroke—something all swimmers have heard of and at least have to try—seems easy now.

How come? Because swimming with just your arms makes as much sense as trying to swing a bat with just your arms instead of winding up the rest of your body first and *then* unleashing all that momentum. Do the latter and you'd be lucky to manage a feeble in-field grounder. Home runs come from the hips. So do swim trophies.

Tuning the Engine

And the energy that powers the process in swimming comes from a simple trick of coordinating that whip-cracking energy chain as it unfolds. Let me explain.

A little formula from your high school physics class, $F = M \times A$, probably went right out the window after your final exam. Well, it's time to get it back. When you do, you'll have a new source of swimming power that won't cost you any energy.

"Force equals mass multiplied by acceleration" is what the equation tells us, and back then even those dozing in the back of the room knew that if either value on the right side of the equals sign went up, the resultant force would go up too. So in this case there are two ways to increase the force. One is by keeping mass the same and increasing acceleration—in other words, don't put more of your body into it, just move your arms faster. If you want to waste energy that's the very way to do it, since energy expenditure balloons as a *cube* of any increase in muscle speed. To move your arms twice as fast takes eight (2^3) times more work.

But what if you turn this around? What if your stroke power could somehow go way up and the effort stay pretty much the same? Couldn't you swim much faster without getting tired? You could and you can. It's done by increasing the M in the formula. Simply move more of your body mass all at once when you stroke. Your arms go at the same speed (perhaps you can even slow them a bit), but now your entire torso is powering them. Feel that new force. Make your hips the first part of the body to move in each stroke, and watch your power grow.

In other words, let your hips set your stroke rhythm, since they're the core of the movement when you're doing it right. Try to set it with your arms instead and they'll quickly go off on their own, breaking the chain and essentially disconnecting themselves from their engine. If you were a car, your transmission would be gone. Lead with your hips instead, and your stroke will be both rhythmic and powerful. Your arms will be happy to follow.

They're Not Hands Anymore: They're Anchors

"Well and good," I hear the mutters, "the hands aren't important. They don't pull us along through the water the way we've been taught since grade school. But they must do *something*. What?" Don't worry. I'm not advocating hands-free swimming. But since they account for perhaps as little as 10 percent of your overall efficiency, I've left the hands for last. As I've said over and over, swimming isn't complicated. Swimming *instruction* is complicated. And that's partly because it's usually delivered by the dumptruck load, all at once and with no priorities. Try to concentrate too early on what your hands are doing, for example, and you'll divert concentration from the far more important body movements. Once your streamlining and balance and rhythmic power are well under way, however, you're entitled to wonder how to best use those appendages out on the ends of your arms.

The best thing you can do is leave them there—not only on your arms but in the water. Several times earlier, I challenged the outmoded notion that you pull water back with your hands. You don't. Now's the time to reply to the obvious question: Then what *do* you do with them? And my answer is, *make them stand still*. Anchor your hands in the water, which is precisely what all great natural freestylers do.

Alexander Popov, since 1992 the world's most dominant sprint freestyler, does even better than that. On every stroke, he takes his hand out *ahead* of where it entered. After he slices his hand in, he grabs and holds the water, using his "grip" to slide his body past his hand, almost as if he had grabbed a rung on a submerged ladder. Making the hand stand still in the water is one of the key "creating" skills of world-class swimmers, many of whom appear to be born with it. But it's nothing the rest of us can't learn.

I'm sure by now you're not surprised to hear that this too starts with hip roll. But now things get more interesting. Power is power only when it has something to act against, and the hips couldn't roll with nearly as much force if your hand didn't first stabilize your upper body at the beginning of each rotation. So the combination of stretching your arm forward at the beginning of the stroke and leaving it there actually does more than "make your boat longer." First, it keeps you from wasting energy in the puny stroke you'd be able to manage with only weak shoulder muscles to pull and no other power or leverage to speak of. Second, it lets you "load the spring," storing up the energy that you'll release in the stroke to come. Remember that batter cocking his arms and shoulders, coiling away from the pitcher before leading into his swing with a hip turn? The golfer's and tennis player's back-swing is the same kind of energy bank, storing muscle tension in the torso that will later be released in the swing, like pulling a bowstring taut before shooting the arrow.

Same thing in your stroke. Your hand enters the water and reaches forward just beneath the surface—and I mean *reaches,* like stretching for something barely beyond your fingertips on a high shelf. Next, with your hand as far out as it can possibly go and your body rolling onto its side, your arm anchors itself into position. Now, with the torso moving and the arm fixed, your upper body becomes increasingly taut, just like the golfer's backswing. And just like the golfer, you're storing up that energy for the action to come—the drive off the tee, the roll of the hips.

Alexander Popov knows just what it feels like. And if you'll walk over to the wall for a minute, you can too. Face the wall and reach up with, say, your right hand, sliding it as far up as you can. Now rotate and lift your elbow slightly off the surface. You'll feel a stretch in the muscles surrounding your armpit. Turn your left hip and shoulder about 45 degrees away from the wall and you'll feel tension building in the powerful latissimus muscle (in your back, below the armpit)—not on the weak shoulder muscles. That's Popov beginning his stroke.

And that's why you grab the water and hold on, just as you resisted the air on your hand out the car window. With practice, you can keep that sense of pressure constant and steady throughout the whole pull.

So there you have it. Jerk your hand back immediately after plunging it in and you've started an exercise in futility as it slips water from one end of the stroke to the other. Bald tires on an icy road. Instead, slip your hand in, anchor it to get ready for the pull, and keep your grip as you move your arm down and back using robust body-roll muscles, not weak shoulder muscles. Welcome to the world of studded snow tires, a V-8, and four-wheel drive to boot.

But still, watch your traction. Tune in to how fast your hands are moving as they pull. Compare the speed of your hands pulling back with the speed of your body moving forward. If they're going faster, you're slipping, not gripping. Your hands should never move faster than your body. Keep practicing until they don't.

Tuning the Engine

One final heresy. Your hand gets from here to there just fine by following a straight line. So if any of the white-coated swimming theoreticians come after you with their clipboards and pointers, sputtering about "S-strokes" and "insweeps" and "outsweeps" and "pitches," tell them you don't sweep and you're not a pitcher. Tell them you simply pull your hand in a straight line back under your body (right down the center of the body, of course) and through the hips. If it was good enough for Johnny Weissmuller, it's good enough for the rest of us. Don't even bother about slicing your hand back outside the hips as you finish. Just press straight through. If your hips are moving as they're supposed to, they'll just roll to the side, conveniently out of the way.

But remember: first a sleek boat, then a powerful engine, and only after that a good propeller. Don't spend more than 10 percent or so of your available training time fussing with perfect use of the hands. They're a footnote at the end of the line, and you want to start at the beginning where the most important action is. And conveniently, that's how the drills are organized for you. First things first.

So let's have a look.

Some Nerve!—
A Whole New Way to Train

By now, it's probably clear that if you expected this book to give you one "workout of champions" after another, you've come to the wrong place. In fact, as a professional swim coach, I can tell you this: If there's one thing practically guaranteed to break down your form and bring improvement to a halt, it's a *workout*.

Think about it. Workouts, by conventional definition, mean working harder or longer to train your heart and lungs and muscles to ignore exhaustion. That means more laps, or harder laps, or both—fatigue by design. The point of these conventional workouts is to do all you can to tire yourself out; then, when you've succeeded in making yourself tired, all those crucial refinements you've been working on so consciously to balance, streamline, and lengthen yourself go right back out the window. The moment your concentration wavers or your resolve weakens even a little bit, you're back to just churning along.

When it comes to your swimming, you can change a poor stroke only by *refusing to swim that way* even once more. Not one stroke. Ever again. But the change doesn't come naturally. So even though the Total Immersion program doesn't throw workouts at you, you can be sure there's still plenty of work to do. That's because, as we've already said, the techniques you'll need to make a dramatic difference in your swimming—dynamic balance, front-quadrant swimming, swimming on your side—are things you just don't do naturally or instinctively. You have to make a conscious decision to swim that way, and even when you have, they'll still be foreign sensations, alien commands traveling along your nervous system, movements that feel funny at first. Your challenge is to change that, to make them second nature. This means that if you want to go beyond just understanding how to swim with maximum efficiency, if you want to make it the way you swim *all the time,* an absolute habit, you have to *practice* specific stroke modifications. And practice, and practice. Think of it as a new kind of training, training that targets the nervous system instead of the aerobic system.

Don't worry. This isn't a thinly disguised "consolation prize" alternative for people without the youth or the power or the genetics or the hour-upon-hour of time to do "real" workouts. It is, in fact, the way the true champions who understand their sport train themselves. And Alexander Popov, the fastest swimmer in the world today, has used extraordinary efficiency to continue winning world championships for an unheard-of eleven years, as he won two world titles in 2003.

For nearly five years, from 1988 to 1992, the American swimmer Matt Biondi had a hammerlock on that title. He deserved it. Biondi swam more efficiently than any of his rivals and was undefeated in his specialty events. During the 1992 Olympics, with Biondi having already announced it would be his last meet, Popov seemed the heir apparent. For several years his coach had videotaped and studied Biondi, using the champion's stroke—the world's most efficient—as a model for his rising star. Coach and swimmer worked tirelessly to master Biondi-like movements.

The showdown came in Barcelona, in the final of the 50-meter free. That event is the ultimate efficiency laboratory, the purest sprint event of them all—one length, no turns, over in maybe 20 seconds. Popov and Biondi stood on the blocks in adjacent lanes in the middle of the eight-man final heat, the gun went off, and the field streaked down the pool. Popov touched first in 21.8 seconds, Biondi right behind at 22.0 seconds. A new Olympic champion had been crowned. But what most amazed analysts was that Popov had not only beaten Biondi by a comfortable margin, he had beaten him thoroughly at Biondi's longest suit—stroke efficiency. Popov had taken 34 strokes, Biondi 37. The time gap may have been just 1 percent, but the three-stroke difference, an *efficiency gap* of nearly 10 percent between the world's two best sprinters, was nearly inconceivable.

It was just the beginning of a new efficiency standard. In the years since, Popov has continued to dominate the sprint events, raising the bar again and again for efficiency and speed. No swimmer on the horizon threatens his stranglehold on the sprint because Popov can swim at startling speeds with much less effort. While everyone else is working furiously, the supremely efficient Popov just seems to be gliding majestically along.

The lesson this champion can teach the rest of us is that it might not have happened at all. Had he simply swum as others did, obsessed with moving briskly up and down the pool for several hours a day—working out—he would have developed less efficient stroke habits and turned into just another swimmer in the pack—albeit a very good pack. Instead he was trained to practice precise technique so it became utter habit. On race day, as his oxygen debt mounts, heart rate soars, and muscles throb, along with his opponents'; everyone else's form breaks down—if only a little bit; his doesn't, and even that modest edge is enough to win every time. His sterling performances are proof of the victory of *practice* over training, of having a nervous system that's at least as well trained as your aerobic system—working smart rather than working out.

Learning Versus Training: How We Build a Skill

The Total Immersion learning system has outperformed all other methods of teaching adults to swim because it's the only one that teaches new skills the way we learn them best—in small pieces. As far as your body is concerned, the job of pumping up an arm muscle is altogether different from teaching that arm muscle to move in an efficient swimming stroke. Skills involve feelings, habits, movements that feel awkward at first and must be made to feel natural. So learning a skill is best organized into a step-by-step process that breaks the big job down into bite-size parts, then recombines them so gradually that each step is easy to master. And the most effective way to tell if you've got it all right is by feel. Every movement you'll be asked to practice in this program is designed to give even the newest swimmer a taste of what the key parts of the swimming stroke *feel* like to an elite athlete. Up to now, every swimming expert has told you how the strokes of an Olympic swimmer *look*. But looks are hard to mimic. Feelings are much easier.

However, just doing the same thing over and over won't make you an expert at anything either—including the freestyle swim stroke. We've all heard of the hapless gentleman wandering aimlessly down

New York City's 57th Street carrying a violin case, finally stopping a passerby to ask, "Excuse me, but how do I get to Carnegie Hall?"

The sardonic reply: "Practice! Practice! Practice!"

Snappy but only half true. Suppose he *did* practice, but without hearing. What if he just scraped his bow over the strings each day no matter what squawks came out, happy that he was getting his arm muscles in shape so he could spend even more time scraping out ugly sounds the next day?

Ridiculous? Don't answer until you're absolutely sure that's not how you—and probably most of the people you know—have been practicing your own swimming for years. Musicians dedicate monumental amounts of rehearsal to produce beautiful sounds, but the quality of their practice time matters to them far more than the quantity. So it should be for swimmers. Practice, we must come to understand, merely makes permanent whatever you happen to be practicing. Good *or* bad.

If you're like most swimmers, making deposits in your aerobic bank account is your main concern. And of course you know that you do that by keeping your heart working in the aerobic range, usually for an hour or so. In essence, a swim workout creates extra heartbeats. If your aerobic training range is 120 beats per minute and your walking-around heart rate is 80, an hourlong workout will create 2,400 extra heartbeats. A perfectly good return on your investment in a nontechnical sport like running. But not in swimming.

In the water, you're ringing up a far more important tally during the course of those 2,400 heartbeats, and that tally is the 2,000 or so strokes you take. Each one leaves a faint impression on your central nervous system, forming a pattern of movement—a *habit*. If you've been swimming for a few years, those stroke habits have become pretty strong. Now stop and think: Since the 2,400 "fitness" heartbeats impact only about 30 percent of your swimming performance while the 2,000 "skill" strokes affect about 70 percent, as we said earlier, which one deserves more of your attention? Right. You're beginning to think like a Total Immersion swimmer already, and you're getting ready to see swimming as a matter of muscle memory, not muscle power.

Muscle memory is what coaches call familiar, habitual patterns of movement. Thanks to muscle memory, you can ride a bike, tie your shoelaces, and type on a computer without stopping and thinking about it. Once you learn a skill well, you can just let your muscles take over. Unfortunately, they'll take over just as aggressively if you've learned a skill badly. And if you think they're interested in giving up those habits, think again.

Muscle memory is like an old vinyl LP that has been played hundreds of times. The stylus, tracking in the record's grooves over and over, gradually wears them deeper. In sports, your muscles and nervous system become more and more "grooved" to automatically execute a movement the same way. Fine if your stroke is efficient. Not fine if it's not. Practiced for long enough, a bad stroke becomes almost immune to change.

Almost immune. But it can be done. What it takes to break old, inefficient habits so new, efficient ones can take their place is the determination to first erase, then replace. You have to make sure that every one of those 2,000 strokes in your workout hour is as much as possible like the economical strokes of skilled swimmers. Settle for less and you're training to become a less accomplished swimmer.

So why do most lap-and-fitness swimmers—and even medal-hungry competitive athletes with coaches—spend most of their pool time working out, trying to improve their physiology with *more* laps or *harder* laps or less rest between repeats? They're on a downhill road. Faltering concentration, fatigue, trying to keep pace with the clock or keep up with another swimmer, will all gradually erode their efficiency. They end up practicing their mistakes.

Start your change today. Begin your transformation from a strictly workout swimmer to a *practice* swimmer. As a workout-only swimmer, strokes were just something that got you from one end of the pool to the other. Laps *were* the point. The tally was sacred. As a practice swimmer you'll realize that each stroke is an investment in your swimming future, each lap a chance to either build your stroke into a well-oiled machine for carrying you fast and far or to break it down into a laborious mess. A practice swimmer works no harder, instead squeezing more good out of the same—or even less—effort.

And while all this is going on, a curious thing will happen to your muscle strength, just as it happened to Alexander Popov's. Even though strength is no longer your holy grail, it will grow, but it will be the muscles that move you most efficiently growing stronger. Popov got to be the best in the world by *practicing*. And while he was doing that, his muscles grew fit enough to break world records. To get the most from your physiology, be less concerned with how many yards you swim and more concerned with how many yards your body travels each time you take a stroke. You'll still get the extra 2,400 heartbeats and your muscles will still get a workout. What can you lose?

Make Those 2,400 Heartbeats Work for You

During TI Weekend Workshops, after patiently explaining for hours that swimming is 70 percent mechanical efficiency and only 30 percent fitness, that practice is more valuable than workout, and urging participants to regard fitness as "something that happens to you while you're practicing good technique," we still expect curiosity over just how fit a swimmer needs to be. Someone always asks: "Yeah, but how many yards a week do I need to be ready for a 1500-meter triathlon swim leg?"

Fitness *is* important, we tell them, very important, but not for the reasons you've probably thought. The reason you want to be in the best possible shape is not to be a powerful athlete but a precision one—so you can keep using your high-level technique over longer distances, at higher speeds and higher heart rates. That's the reason our program starts in the easiest possible way: with efficient movements, over short distances, at low speeds, and at low heart rates. You gradually build your capacity to *hold that form* longer, harder, and faster. Sounds a lot like race preparation, doesn't it?

So the big role of fitness is to help you hold your form. But all fitness is not alike. I compete in Masters swimming on a semiregular basis. When I do, I usually target a regional or national open-water championship in the summer, devoting several months to intense, focused preparation. After the summer I cut back on my swimming and start running several times a week for a change of pace. And every time I do, no matter how hard I've worked and how well-conditioned

I've gotten myself in the water, my muscles rudely remind me that as a runner, I'm a rookie.

It's the same thing that happens right in the pool when you switch strokes. If I've done mostly freestyle training, I'll be lucky to feel good for the first half of a breaststroke race. The second half crumbles into a desperate struggle against muscle fibers that are quitting one after the other because they simply haven't been trained. Breaststroke muscles are different from freestyle muscles. If they're new to the job, they won't do it for very long.

Now let's cut the distinction finer still. You even use different muscles for swimming freestyle with good form than you do with poor form. Train sloppily and your better-conditioned poor-form muscles will be in great shape. You can guess what happens next. Come race time—or even a longer-than-usual workout—your well-intentioned brain will give your body the right pep talk ("Okay, now, let's really hold good form here!"), but if you haven't trained the muscles it's talking to, their answer will quickly be "Forget it." You'll be stuck with "sloppy-swimming" power.

Nobody can get away with that whether they go for speed or distance. Neither top speed nor effective endurance can be achieved with pinch-hitting stand-in muscles. If you swim the 100-yard freestyle in a Masters meet in 60 seconds and would like to do it in 58, your primary goal is to train yourself to stay efficient as you move everything faster. You'll get those two seconds and more. Or say you do a 1500-meter triathlon swim leg in 36 minutes and would like to do it in 30. Now the strategy is to stay efficient *longer.* If you used to get a shaky stroke at around 300 meters, and can now hold form right through the final

1200, you're going to make a serious dent in that finishing time. None of that happens unless, like Popov, you program your muscles to do it.

And more than your muscles are working to form every stroke. What do you think fires them in the first place? Right. The nervous system. And though this part of the training process is almost always overlooked, the nervous system also stores away everything you do during that hour or so you're in the pool. Lap after lap it selectively recruits muscle "motor units" to move your arms and legs in certain ways, learning as it goes. Just as with the muscles themselves, you're either training it to be habitually efficient or habitually inefficient. Routinely let your efficiency slip over the course of an hour and that's just what your nervous system will be ready to do for you next time and the time after that. It will remember. You need to make sure it remembers what you want it to.

Learning Skills with Success Drills

New triathletes are often amazed that they can pick up a bike after a cycling layoff of twenty years and feel like they never missed a day. No rustiness, no relearning—*zoom!* Off they go. That's because the ability has been there all those years; it's just been in storage. The skill comes out again easily because it's fairly simple—cyclical, rhythmic, hands and feet fixed in place. You don't have to repolish much besides your balance and steering, and that doesn't take long because all the time we spent doing it as kids left a powerful and permanent imprint on our nervous systems. The neural groove on your bike-riding LP is already deep. The needle never jumps. And it's a much simpler tune to play.

Swimming, of course, is nothing like that. Neither is tennis. And though on the surface there seems little to unite those sports, they have far more in common than most athletes—and most of their coaches—realize. In fact, the way to understand how the body best learns a skill and why the Total Immersion training system is so effective at speeding that process along is to watch someone with a good coach learning his or her way around the tennis courts.

First, the basics. Tennis and swimming are both motor-skill sports that also take strength and endurance for success. In swimming, skill and stamina combine to move you up and down the pool faster, farther, and easier. In tennis, skill puts the ball right where you want it, while stamina chases down the return and holds stroke-crippling fatigue at bay.

So you'd think swimmers and tennis players would learn useful training techniques from each other, but they don't. You'd think they'd realize their practices are a lot alike—or should be. But they don't. Swimmers try to improve just by swimming more. But they don't.

Tennis players wise up faster. Many start the same way by "just doing it," digging up a tolerant partner and smacking the ball back and forth. They usually don't get very far that way. In the beginning especially, they spend more time chasing down wayward balls than hitting rallies. It soon dawns that they won't improve much if they can't even keep the ball in play.

So they sign up for lessons with a tennis pro. "Pro," after all, has a nice, crisp ring that sounds so . . . well, so professional. "Coach," as in swimming coach, implies someone who just tells you how to sweat. Too often, both implications are on target, to the great advantage of the tennis player.

A Whole New Way to Train

The tennis pro understands that the most important thing to do for his or her students is teach them, not train them. They need to master skills that will make them competitive on the court, and the pro needs to help those students learn faster and with the least possible confusion. That means starting off with the simplest possible movements—small segments of the basic strokes. In the forehand lesson, for example, the student simply stands with his feet planted in one spot, racquet held back, while the teacher lobs the ball so that it bounces up softly at waist height and practically into the strings of the racquet all by itself. A successful return is guaranteed.

Even so, the first ten or twenty are awkward, mechanical, erratic. Gradually they grow smoother, more accurate, more consistent. The learning and sorting-out have begun as muscles and nerves catalogue and memorize the difference between swings that work and swings that don't. If a ball flies out of bounds, the student "erases" that swing from muscle memory. If it ends up just where she wants it, she replays that one over and over. Not only can she see her successes and failures, she can feel them. The jolting *thwwoong* of a vibrating mis-hit rockets right up her forearm, while the precise *pong* of the racket's "sweet spot" feels and sounds solid and true. Each time, the experience is "written to disk" in the nervous system where, eventually, hundreds and thousands of such "experiments" in movement skill begin to build a vast neuromuscular database of experiences. Only one or two of those resulted in hitting a good ball, of course, so gradually the student's muscles figure out how to do just those. That's when the pro sees something especially rewarding: The returns are now virtually automatic. Step one is complete. The basic forehand has become encoded in muscle memory.

Learning any new motor skill is a similar problem-solving, trial-and-error exercise. But too much error can be so discouraging that enthusiasm goes right down the drain, and with it the chance to improve. The secret is to practice something you can do, not something you can't. An easily mastered basic skill becomes the springboard for a more advanced one, and so on. You see results every step of the way.

That's why the pro waits until step two to hit the ball around, making it seem a little more like a real game of tennis. This should be fun, the student thinks, until her nice, new, smooth, and coordinated basic stroke turns to shreds again as she now tries to second-guess where the ball is going to be before she can figure out how to meet it with her racquet. Think for a minute what's behind just getting to the ball. Mind and muscles watch the ball's trajectory and direction, compute where it's going to land, rush to that spot, and get the feet and torso into position to swing before the ball arrives. Only then do they get to use that now-familiar basic skill—returning the ball. Moreover, they now need a unique program for each shot depending on where the ball lands and how fast it's going. It may take dozens of such lessons just to develop a rudimentary tennis game. Obviously, the only way to make sense out of the wilderness of skill building is by a stepwise system of learning, and practice that's organized to take the student through it.

Which is exactly what's been missing from most swimming instruction. Swimming coaches spend so much time training and so little time teaching that few have ever really thought about how to break down their equally complex sport into a series of fundamentals that can be taught step by step. Instead, their stroke advice comes in scattershot bursts, not in a series of "success lessons" that can be mastered quickly and that automatically lay the groundwork for the next skill. Their swimmers spend too much time swimming the whole stroke, never quite able to achieve fluency in all its parts. With Total Immersion, we teach like the tennis pro instead.

With one important difference. Tennis players have a big advantage over swimmers: They can see their results, and they can see them right away. Ball goes right or ball goes wrong. Swimmers have nothing that obvious to guide them. Unless someone is standing poolside bellowing at you like a coach as you swim, you have to rely on how things feel inside your water capsule. So your skill-building drills must be designed with "feeling feedback," letting your nerve endings be your coach.

Let's go back to the most critical improvement you can make—getting your body balanced and stable. It doesn't come naturally, it doesn't feel natural, and new swimmers who balance by instinct are as rare as a balanced federal budget. It takes most people years of trial-and-error practice to figure out balance on their own, if they ever do. Our skill drills skip trial and error entirely and, by telling you what feeling you should aim for, put you through each critical step of the process quickly. You can learn balance, for instance, in thirty minutes or less. Drill by drill, cutting out hour after hour of dead-end experimentation, we put the whole learning process into high gear.

So that's swimming, the Total Immersion way. Realizing now that your skills carry you a lot farther than your fitness, you don't work out anymore—you practice. And you repeat to yourself as often as necessary: *"Fitness is something that happens to me while I'm practicing good technique."* And practicing, and practicing, because now you also know that old habits die hard, especially old muscle habits. If you've been swimming without instruction for several years, in fact, you've probably had so much practice at inefficient swimming that your body is an absolute champion at it. To learn a better way of swimming, you have to unlearn the one you're stuck with, which means never doing it again. Every length you swim with poor form makes it harder to improve.

And the way we'll make sure you've swum your last length with poor form is to use the same step-by-step strategy that tennis pros perfected long ago. There's no reason for racquet sports to be any better than water sports at helping athletes build good technique. Tennis players may have gotten wise sooner, but with Total Immersion, swimmers are now there too.

The tennis program works so well because it meters out a series of easily mastered mini-skills that gradually link together into a smoother, more powerful game. Efficient swimming can now be taught in the same logical, step-by-step process. It all starts with the best friend your swimmer's nervous system ever had: the skill drill. It makes the complex simple, the intimidating comfortable, and the difficult easy. In the next chapter, the mini-skill finally arrives at the pool.

Good-bye, "coach." Welcome to your first lesson with the "swimming pro."

Skill Drills:
The Fastest Way
to a Faster Stroke

Sometimes I think that if we left it up to the experts, the only people who'd dare to get into a swimsuit would be elite athletes with burning Olympic aspirations and children too carefree to have any aspirations at all. Because the "experts" all warn us: An efficient swimming stroke is a prize with a staggering price. So many motions to coordinate! So many ways to go wrong! No wonder it takes countless hours of practice to reach a decent level of skill and smoothness. Why, the grooming of an Olympic-level swimmer usually begins not long after kindergarten—at the age of seven or eight! And even then, for maybe five years, the basic skills are hammered in over and over before the first hints of training for strength and endurance.

Rubbish. For an Olympic aspirant, maybe that's what it takes. But it doesn't have to be that way for the rest of us. And for adults, who generally haven't had that kind of time since they were kids themselves, it simply *can't* be that way. So without professionals to guide them and with few hours to invest, grown-up swimming hopefuls usually just plod through the laps, hoping that as the mileage piles up their strokes will improve. Instead, as we said in the last chapter, they're making things worse by practicing their mistakes. And the more they swim this way, the harder it will become to snap out of it someday. They may finally reach a state that one of my campers wistfully called "terminal mediocrity."

It used to be that your only hope for breaking out of those bad habits was to find a good coach. Not anymore. There are ways you can turn things around and begin learning improved skills all by yourself, methods we'll teach you in the next few chapters.

It all starts with what I call the stroke saver, otherwise known as the skill drill. Think of the skill drill as your personal and powerful Batman against the Joker of bad swimming habits, able to root them out thoroughly, replacing them with sound, new ones almost automatically. The skill drill is—no exaggeration—the quickest and most effective path to masterful swimming. Skill drills are the core of the successful method I've used for over two decades to help swimmers of all ages to improve dramatically. One of the reasons is that the drills are so easy to learn that even inexperienced swimmers can become their own best coaches.

I don't care if you've been frustrated for years. You can dramatically improve your swimming in just hours with these technique drills, a process that has no way of happening when you plod mindlessly up and down the pool practicing your mistakes.

With conventional instruction, the learning process can consume tedious and frustrating months. Drills work by speeding up your learning curve, and that's no small feat. Even excellent swimmers who look like they must have been born with their effortless grace have probably invested months, or more likely years, in polishing that smooth, almost balletlike way of moving. Sometimes a coach's guidance did the trick; in other cases their exceptional intuitions were enough. But either way, the process is the same: Over time, they've hit on breakthrough moments when their stroke feels just right, moments that the body immediately seizes and—just like the body of our tennis pupil—stores in a catalogue of similar how-to-move experiences. Eventually, the catalogue becomes comprehensive enough to produce an extremely smooth and highly efficient way of swimming.

It's a process that never really ends—which is one of the most exciting things about swimming. There's virtually no improvement ceiling when it comes to good technique. Whether you're a beginner just "getting your stroke wet" or an expert looking to medal at a national meet, there's always something left to work on. The refinements just become increasingly subtle. After winning an astounding seven Olympic medals in 1988, Matt Biondi admitted, "I still see every practice as a learning experience because I've come to realize that even now, I only understand about ten percent of what efficient swimming is all about."

But trial and error is a very time-consuming way to pick up an involved skill like swimming—as any self-taught tennis player can tell you. So the Total Immersion method takes this haphazard and painfully slow process and organizes it for you. The result is a step-by-step system of drills selected so any swimmer can re-create, in an organized, convenient, and reliable way, his or her own "flashes of learning" to put into the catalogue. Suddenly you can capture those elusive feelings of being "in sync" whenever you want instead of stumbling onto them now and again by accident. Best of all, you can practice them again and again.

Still, as all the king's horses, all the king's men, and Humpty-Dumpty all found out, parts are just parts until you put them back together again. When you go back to swimming the whole stroke after polishing pieces of it in your drills, your body reassembles them naturally into a much-improved whole. Your nerve endings have done your learning for you by taking "snapshots" of sensations that elite swimmers feel consistently as they knife through the water, and assembling them into a complete photo album: your stroke.

Now, if you suspect that we're really just drawing out the learning process with all this pulling apart and putting back together, I'll let you in on the four powerful physical facts that make skill drills such a potent stroke-improvement tool:

1. *Fact: Your Muscles Need a Dose of Amnesia.* Muscles have memories, as we said. Habits are powerful. And that's just what the stroke you've been using for years has become—a habit. Probably not a good one either. And because you've been struggling for so long, your muscles have become very good at moving like that. They'd prefer to keep right on doing it, in fact.

Stroke drills are powerful enough to break that cycle because they're disguised. They're so different from your normal motion that your muscle doesn't recognize the movement and insist you do it in the same old way. You practice new skills on a neuromuscular blank slate without having to erase anything first.

2. *Fact: Small Pieces Are Easier to Swallow.* Learning specialists tell us we pick up skills faster by breaking a complex movement series into manageable segments for practice. Because the swimming stroke is made up of so many finely coordinated parts, it's virtually impossible to digest the whole thing. So our Total Immersion stroke drills are "bite-size,"

reducing the whole stroke into a series of mini-skills, each of which can be quickly mastered. Then you simply reassemble these building blocks into a new, more efficient stroke. Each drill teaches a key skill, and we present them in the order the body best understands. It's like putting up a building: The first drill is the foundation, each succeeding drill adds a floor, and mastery of each step gives you the key to solving the next one.

3. *Fact: Instead of Trial and Error, It's Trial and Success.* Drills stack the learning deck completely in your favor. You can't lose. Because mini-skills can be mastered quickly and easily, you begin practicing smooth movements right away. The more you practice each smooth movement, the more it becomes your new habit and crowds out the sloppy old one. And the less time you spend swimming with your sloppy old one, the faster you learn to swim better. That string of successes boosts your motivation and self-confidence—and studies have shown that happens faster when you believe in what you're doing.

4. *Fact: It's Language the Body Understands.* Telling a muscle what to do is a little like teaching French to your poodle: You get rapt attention but not much retention. Conventional stroke instruction suffers from the same weakness. It's too rational. It tries to get to your muscles through your mind, even though muscles really don't respond all that well to being lectured. Think about it. First you have to hear, or possibly read, a description of what you're going to attempt. Next, you try to figure out what the movement will feel like. Then you instruct your muscles to imitate that feeling. Finally, you ask yourself if you got it right. If you didn't, you try it again a little differently.

Skill Drills

Drills bypass all those vague translations. They simplify—and accelerate—the learning process. From the very beginning, you teach your body how it should *feel* when you swim well.

The great part is, skill drills are self-adjusting. The more you need them, the better they'll work for you. When beginners practice them they learn basic skills in big chunks and rough edges get smoothed off quickly. Experienced swimmers, doing the same drills, tune in naturally to far more subtle refinements, bringing a higher degree of polish to skills they already have.

And the more you have to learn, the more you should drill—up to four times as much as your normal swimming if you really have your work cut out for you. It may be the only way to make headway against bad habits so hardened through the years that they're all but concrete. Think of it this way: Every lap of drilling, which you can learn to do well quickly, is positive reinforcement for your swimming. Every lap of swimming may pull you back toward old habits. I tell my workshop pupils to ask themselves: "How much swimming can I *suffer*, as I try to teach my body new skills?"

And though every swimmer is different, drills work for most with incredible speed. *Everyone* I've taught them to has improved. I can't think of any other swim instruction method that can claim that. And they'll work even faster if you:

1. *Think Before You Swim.* Every drill is a problem-solving exercise, and nothing beats the old-fashioned virtues of patience and persistence when you're trying to solve a problem. With each new drill—and every time you do refresher drilling the first month or two following

this program—take these steps: *First, a few repetitions* just to remind your muscles of the problem the drill is meant to solve, such as moving your head and torso together as you roll your body to breathe. *Next, several repetitions* to work out the solution. *Finally, several more repetitions* spent "memorizing" that solution so it comes naturally. Now you "own" it.

2. Do It with Feeling. These drills get your muscles talking to your brain instead of the other way around. If your brain is listening, it's going to learn what the motion or skill you're practicing feels like when it's done right. And when it learns that, it can start to replay it automatically. Feels right, *is* right; and the mind-muscle connection begins to work more smoothly. So the first few times you work on any new drill, *stick with it for at least ten to fifteen minutes* to firmly imprint the new sense into your memory so the brain can eventually go by sensation rather than by thought. Don't be rigid. Experiment with subtle adjustments. See how much control you really have and what happens when you alter these new movements even slightly. Eventually you want your body to take over from your mind, automatically doing what at first required all your concentration.

3. Don't Drill Yourself into a Hole. Marathon drill sets can easily do more harm than good, a case of too much of a good thing. If you're tired and can't concentrate, you won't drill well, and drills build good skills only when they're done well. *Practice them in 25-yard repeats, resting ten to fifteen seconds between.* Every rep should feel a little smoother and more relaxed, a little more precise and economical. If not, reread the instructions or go back to the previous drill and polish that one up before returning to the one that's giving you trouble.

Skill Drills

4. *Take Your Drills Out for a Test Swim.* Work no more than ten to fifteen minutes at a time on a new drill. Then *alternate drill lengths with swim lengths,* trying to make each swim length a little more efficient—taking fewer strokes—and a little easier. Compare your drill and your stroke. What felt better in the drill? Good. Try to get more of that feeling into your stroke. When you're pressing your buoy, for example, your hips and legs will suddenly feel light as they skim the surface instead of dragging along behind you. Focus on that. See how much of it you can feel when you're swimming. Think of it as your chance to do a virtual-reality lap with a Popov stroke. And keep at it. Lasting improvement won't happen instantaneously.

5. *If the Fin Fits . . .* Here's a paradox. Drills are designed to get your body so well balanced that you won't need much of a kick to swim well. A weak kick won't slow you down anymore. But you will need a bit of propulsion from your legs to drill well. Your body's moving slower—and lower in the water as a result—while drilling than when you swim. A bit of kick helps compensate. If yours is weak, you'll waste so much energy struggling for the right body position that you won't have much left to drill with. Slip on a pair of fins, and you'll be able to pay attention to what matters—the fine points in each drill. By the way, for skill work bladed fins are far better than the cut-off, so-called speed fins, particularly if your ankles don't flex easily yet.

Drill-and-Swim: Some Assembly Required

In my program, skill drills are little short of magic—absolutely the best way to improve. But they can do that only if you fit them properly into the puzzle of the whole swimming stroke. And just as particular puzzle pieces have to fit into the whole in a particular way, drills don't go just anywhere in your swimming workouts. Drill without a plan and you could miss the whole point.

Drills, you see, can be the potato chips of swim training: so addictive you begin to lose your appetite for other things. Things like swimming. I've seen people become absolutely terrific drillers and do little to nothing for their swimming stroke in the process. They've let good drilling become an end in itself.

That's not necessarily bad if all you want is to be fit. Drills can be a workout all by themselves, sometimes more of a workout than swimming would have been. In fact, you could easily stay in great shape doing nothing but drills without ever taking a single conventional stroke. But wouldn't that be a little like carefully assembling all the parts to a classic MG and then never building the car? Yes, drills can be fun, and they do offer scenic byways to the monotony of the turnpike—swimming the black line back and forth and back and forth—but let's not get carried away.

Drills build skills, but they build them best if you integrate and alternate them with swimming in an organized way. Remember, drills are: (1) the simplest way to teach your muscles new movement patterns; and (2) the best way to turn up the volume on feelings that tell you when you're swimming well. Alternating with swimming will give your drills the most powerful influence over your stroke. They'll give you a *sensory target,* a feeling you're looking for. And when you have a feeling you're looking for, you can better focus your practice.

Your progress in this program will be steady and reliable because we've organized those sensory exercises into logical sequences, just the way your body wants to learn them. Each sense skill builds on the one before it. You can't lengthen your stroke, for example, until you've first gotten yourself balanced.

Be patient. Drill-swim will work. It can't fail, in fact, because it employs natural learning methods. Your body is a brilliantly intuitive instrument, with a faultless sense of what it needs—given enough information. As you drill and swim, you'll sense what works best and gradually capture that and make it your own. But remember: This learning instrument works best when allowed to learn at its own pace. You didn't pick up all your bad habits overnight and you're not going to pick up new ones overnight either. Just one repetition of a new drill may start the learning process, may even begin tracing a faint neurological imprint that will make the next repetition easier and more natural. But real skill requires that the groove be cut deeply through many repetitions, each done the same way.

So don't try to force-feed yourself. Patient, persistent repetition of the drills to get the feeling right, alternating with swim laps where you take that feeling and put it right into your stroke, is the best way to let drills work their magic. Use short repeats and short sets. Fresh muscles train well. Fatigue—mental or physical—brings sloppiness. And sloppiness is what you'll be practicing once you're tired or bored. Just 25 yards of a drill, followed by 25 yards of swimming, followed by a short rest, will give you the highest-quality practice. Give it all you've got for maybe ten minutes or so. Then give your brain a rest by doing something that requires less concentration—a few laps of stroke counting, for example, to see how much more efficient you've become.

And as judges are fond of reminding lawyers, you need to keep to the point. Don't work on one thing in your drill and drift off into thinking about something else during the swimming you do right afterward. Focus, focus, focus, in drills *and* in swimming. If you worked on pressing your buoy while drilling, don't start thinking about hip roll on your swim length. You'll never finish anything.

And I'll go even further. Your drill guidelines in this book's swim lessons suggest five or six points to concentrate on in each drill. That's about four or five too many to do all at the same time. You can think about exactly one, and one only, with enough clarity and focus to do it well. Get greedy, go for two or three at the same time, and they'll all get fuzzy. You won't do any of them well as your concentration leapfrogs all around. Instead, force yourself to do a little drill triage, with my permission. Decide which points you clearly feel make the greatest difference in your stroke and spend more drill lengths thinking about those. Keep the exact same point in mind on your next swim length. (See the appendix for sample practices that do this.) Focus, focus, focus.

And gradually, when you're ready, wean, wean, wean. Stretch farther and farther the distance you can swim with better form before heading back to the drills for a reminder. For that *is* how it will happen, maybe three steps (or strokes) forward, one step back. In the beginning, you see, that neurological tracery is still faint. It may take you three or four drill lengths to even get a clear sense of what it is you're practicing, and it may be all you can do just to hold that sensation for one full swim length once you get it. So your ratio of drill lengths to

Skill Drills

swim lengths could easily be as high as 3:1 or 4:1. As you continue practicing, though, your body will get it faster and faster. Eventually, one drill length might groove that feeling back into muscle memory firmly enough to shift right over to a swim length.

Little by little, you'll work up to two lengths before your form begins to wobble and need a drill refresher. Then three lengths. Then. . . . But be patient at stretching the distance. Eventually, you'll be able to take the new, improved you for much longer cruises. Feels good, doesn't it? Well, congratulations. Your old habits are on the run, your muscles are now beginning to remember the right stuff, and the stroke that was holding you back is losing its grip on you. Now it's time to pry loose a few more of its fingers. Hang on to your concentration but take off the training wheels. Let's start some full-stroke swimming.

Come to Your Senses.
Swim by Feel

If "sensory skill practice" sounds to you like an ad on late-night cable TV for an adult videotape, I need a minute of your time before we go any further.

Because SSP, as I call it, is actually something a good deal more important—well, more important to an improvement-minded swimmer, certainly. It's nothing less than the capstone, the finishing touch, on the whole Total Immersion learning process. Each Total Immersion drill focuses on some aspect of swimming described in chapters 2 through 4. Each drill, in turn, heightens the kinesthetic, or sensory, experience of how "right swimming" *feels.* In SSP, we practice swimming while focused on that feeling.

In sensory skill practice you take all the ingredients of an efficient stroke, the ones you so meticulously developed in your skill drills and rehearsed in your drill-swim sessions, and make them permanent. Automatic. Yours. Good form that your body follows instinctively, free at last of those nagging reminder lectures from your brain. That daunting mental punch list—Am I pressing my buoy enough? Is my body long? What about hip roll? Did I reach for the far end?—is edited down to a simple and smooth body check: Does it *feel* right?

Teach your senses what "right swimming" *feels* like, you see, and they'll take over and do more to help you hold good swimming form than a video camera ever could. Automatically and accurately.

The challenge is figuring out how to take full advantage of your new movements. At this point they're like individual sheets of music that you can play well in whatever order they turn up on the music stand. But if they're ever going to become a concerto, they must follow a certain coherent sequence.

So what we do in sensory skill practice is to arrange your skills in a logical order and "play" them that way, since some let you unlock others, like opening a series of nested Russian dolls. For though I preach consistently throughout this book that the way to become a better swimmer is to cut swim time and drill, drill, drill, there comes a point when you have to swim, swim, swim. But what a difference now! You've gotten over your black-line fever. The odometer no longer rules your life. It's not how long or how far but how well. You finally know what it feels like when you've got it right. Your job now is to make sure it always feels that way from now on.

Don't be surprised if your body at first has trouble trusting this "swim by feel" approach. After all, it's just the opposite of what many of us were told to do by our school coaches. Back then, we worked on *ignoring* instead of paying attention. Face it: The way most of us were schooled, if you took athletics seriously you didn't shrink from getting falling-down tired. And a good coach, in those days, was someone who could help your mind wander off to something other than how miserable you were feeling, to "disassociate" from the workout so you'd forget how exhausted you were and manage to keep on going just a little longer and a little longer after that. Like my peers—and probably like yours—when I paid any attention at all to what my body was doing, it began and ended with wondering how well I was using my hands to paddle.

So that was the extent of my technical focus when I came back to regular swim training in my late thirties. And today, it very probably is still yours.

When it gradually became clear that body positioning is so much more important to effective swimming than endurance or strength, I knew I would have to completely reverse my idea of training. Instead of *telling* my body what to do, I would start *listening* to it as it reported in from thousands upon thousands of nerve endings and informed the brain—as it had always tried to do—what was working well and what wasn't. Now, though, instead of ignoring all this information, I would guide it into the smoothest possible technique and focus the lion's share of that attention on my torso—the body's power source—instead of my arms and legs.

My first sensory experiment was with pressing the buoy. As a coach I'd been teaching it to butterfliers for nearly twenty years. Leaning on the chest in that stroke made it conspicuously easier for them to bring their hips up. But it wasn't until around 1990 that it occurred to me that the same principle of lifting the hips and legs to reduce drag might work in freestyle too. As a test, I asked a couple of new swimmers who were struggling especially hard to give it a try. The difference was immediate and so dramatic you didn't need to be a professional coach to be impressed with the results. I realized that it could help my own swimming as well. And probably everyone else's.

But the habits of coaches, even young ones, die just as hard as anyone's. True, those first tentative shifts into greater torso awareness sparked an immediate improvement. But I'd already been swimming for twenty-five years, and long habit kept my mind drifting back to what those hands of mine were doing. The moment I lost concentration, I knew I had also lost body position. The sudden drag on my back half told me so. Obviously, if I wanted to hold on to this improvement, or any other improvement for that matter, I had to figure out a way of making it automatic and instinctive—"in the bank," so to speak. Then I could go on to the next.

So I did what any good athlete would do: worked as hard as I could at nailing that improvement down. What I nailed down instead was the realization that long swims or hard swims simply break down the critical ability to concentrate. They actually give new life to old habits. The only thing that worked was short repeats where I ignored the clock, other swimmers, my hands, and what I might be having for dinner. Just one thing was allowed on the mental table: chest pressure for keeping the hips light. Total sensory absorption. And it worked.

Best of all, it continued to work for every piece of the skill puzzle I wanted to add. In the next two years I packed more efficiency into my stroke than I'd managed to eke out in the previous twenty-five years. You can do the same.

If It Feels Good, Do It. And Do It Some More.

The difference between sensory skill practice and drill-and-swim is the difference between cycling without training wheels and cycling with them. Drill-and-swim is training-wheel swimming: If you start to go wrong and lose your balance or form, you can fall back on the drills for support. Sensory skill practice takes the wheels off for as long as you can leave them off. It challenges you to pedal straight and true, as far as you can go, before starting to wobble again.

Here's how it works. On each drill length, you zeroed in on one specific sensation—light hips and legs, longer body, weightless arm, rolling hips—then held on to it as you swam, like practicing a bar of music over and over. The more lengths you swam that way, the deeper that feeling sank into your neurological memory bank. Eventually, the feeling sank in deeply enough to become your natural stroke.

Or did it? Your objective in sensory skill practice is to find out. Take the same catalogue of desirable sensations and see how far or how fast you really can swim with one or another of them. Consciously practice skillful swimming—and nothing else. Instead of counting laps or racing the clock or another swimmer, you're focused on using each lap and every stroke to imprint specific skills more and more deeply, more and more permanently.

In a sense, sensory skill practice puts the finishing touches on the learning process. In step one, you learned new ways of moving using drills. In step two, you integrated those movements into your swim stroke. Now you're testing your ability to swim consistently better—with consistently less thought. It's the drill work without the drills. Drills teach you what these sensations feel like; then you take them into your stroke and simply practice *feeling like that* as you swim.

But this is far more than just "mop-up" work. Many of these movements, remember, are alien to our nervous systems at first, so almost any workout will eventually break down your new and still-fragile form. Frankly, it will take all your patience and determination to make the new form natural and instinctive. But it will be worth it.

The best news is that you can count on the fingers of one hand all the drag-minimizing SSP movements you need to practice, as you'll see in the following list of five. The "how-to" part sounds a lot like the drills, and it is. But now, you're not drilling anymore. "This ain't no practice run," as the saying goes. This is taking the more efficient you and really *swimming* with it:

1. *Swimming Downhill:* This tests how well you're able to press your buoy to improve your balance, bring your butt to the surface, and reduce drag. Learn to do it right, and improvement is instantaneous. Guaranteed.

> **HOLD ON TO THIS SSP FEELING:** Just as you did on the pressing-your-buoy drill, tell yourself you've got to lean on your chest as you swim. You may feel as if you're swimming downhill. That's good. Other swimmers have said it's like someone pressing down on their shoulder blades as they swim. And a runner recognized the feeling from her sport: She felt as though she were leaning forward slightly to balance and brace her body against a punchy headwind. When you get it right, your hips will feel lighter, your kick far easier. In fact, relax your legs completely so they can simply follow along. Keep leaning and skimming the water. If you do it consciously and religiously, you'll eventually do it instinctively.

2. *Swimming with a Weightless Arm:* The key to front-quadrant swimming, which makes your body taller and faster in the water.

HOLD ON TO THIS SSP FEELING: When you swim downhill, putting all your weight on your buoy, your extended arm should feel virtually weightless as it practically floats out in front of you after it enters the water. Your fingertips thrust effortlessly toward the far end of the pool until you *choose* to apply pressure to your hand and begin the stroke. You also feel elongated—your weightless arm makes you taller each time you stroke, and even taller as you roll to breathe.

3. *Reaching for the Far Wall:* This complements the weightless arm. Some swimmers can't fight the impulse to dive right into the stroke as soon as their hand touches the water. Not good. It makes them shorter, makes them slower, and makes them unbalanced. This breaks that habit.

    HOLD ON TO THIS SSP FEELING: If your hands stubbornly jerk down and back as soon as they enter the water, try this. Pretend every stroke is the last of your lap, the one where you reach out for the pool wall. Swim every stroke of the lap that way. *Reach* for the wall. As you're reaching, feel your shoulder press alongside your jawline. (If it's a breathing stroke, you should feel your ear pressing into the shoulder of the extending arm.) Then, when you can't reach any farther, begin to pull. One more point: Reach *slowly* for the wall; your hand shouldn't be extending any faster than your body is moving forward.

4. *Hand Swapping:* You've learned to extend your arm and lengthen your body, but how long should that "extender" stay out there before

the other hand shows up? Hand swapping tells you when to begin stroking the extended hand as the recovery hand comes around.

HOLD ON TO THIS SSP FEELING: Does it seem like you're waiting to start your stroke just a little longer than you're used to? That's it! The whole point, in fact, is to put off pulling with the extended hand until the other one is just about to reenter the water and take its place in front of your head. As we said, this keeps your body longer—and faster—for more of each stroke cycle. But you won't be able to do it unless your extended arm is weightless, so go back and master that one first if you haven't yet.

You may have to do a little drill to get hand swapping right. "Whoa. Back to drills again?" you protest. "Why are you making me repeat a grade in this swimming school of yours?" Don't worry. This is the hardest to learn of all the sensory skill targets because it involves subtle stroke-timing adjustments, but it's worth mastering because it can greatly increase your stroke length. Practice this sequence—in 25-yard increments—until it begins to feel comfortable.

1. Begin each new stroke when your recovering hand is between elbow and wrist of the extended hand.
2. Begin each stroke when your recovering hand is between shoulder and elbow of the extended hand.
3. Begin each stroke when your recovering hand passes your goggles.
4. Swim silently and count your strokes.

Initially, hand swapping feels exaggerated and unnatural. This four-step practice guides your body into gradually feeling at home with the movement. Cycle over and over through this sequence and you'll soon pinpoint the "sweet spot" in your stroke timing.

5. *Moving Your Midsection:* If swimming on your side still feels awkward and your hips resist your brain's message to roll, practice this one.

> **HOLD ON TO THIS SSP FEELING:** Nothing ambiguous about what to do here. On every stroke, just point your belly button toward the pool side wall on each side. Not literally, of course—you'd need a ball-bearing-mounted spine to roll that far. But with that target, you will move better. And as increased roll begins to feel more natural, you can relax because you'll be doing it without thinking. Just make sure you're always shifting your midsection rhythmically from side to side. Now you're swimming with your powerful hips, not your puny hands. When you want to swim more powerfully yet, put more *snap* into your hip rhythm. When you want to swim faster, put more *speed* into your hip rhythm. Keep it up until your whole sense of stroke rhythm is the rhythm of your midsection moving back and forth, not that of your arms churning.

The most powerful testimony I can give for the effectiveness of sensory skill practice is that I've actually seen it succeed where drill work stumbled. Despite all the wonderful things I've seen drills do for people, some swimmers just have a hard time with them. For one reason or another—poor kick, poor coordination, even anxiety about being in the water—they struggle when they drill, and unfortunately even begin to wonder if they're swimming-student material.

Sensory Skill Practice: Easy Does It

1.   Start by alternating SSP with drill lengths that broadcast the same message. The similarities between the two will give you a clearer and stronger grasp of the exact sensation you're after.

2.   Limit your practice to 25-yard (or single-length) repeats at first. Swim the first half-length without breathing—not to see if you can do without air but because your body will absorb the new sensation faster if it doesn't also have to attend to the mechanics of breathing. Then segue smoothly into normal breathing but stay strongly and narrowly focused on the sensation.

3.   Go slowly. Your body is more sensitive to new sensations when moving gently through the water. You'll have plenty of chance to pile on speed later.

4.   At the end of each length, stop and think a moment about what you just did. If you were swimming downhill, did your hips feel lighter and your kick easier? If you were reaching for the wall, did you feel your body lengthen? If not, go back to the related drill, which will accentuate and clarify the feeling you're trying to create.

5.   Do enough lengths for the sensation to settle in. You'll know when that happens, but I'd look for it at around eight to ten repeats while you're working on something new.

And when you've got all that under your belt, keep your momentum going by:

1.   Gradually lengthening your repeats to 50, 100, perhaps even 200 yards. It's not too ambitious to want to eventually swim a mile or more

with your new efficiency intact, if that's the length of a race you plan to swim.

2.   Blending two sensations in one length (e.g., swim downhill with a weightless arm, or reach for the wall with a weightless arm, or swim downhill moving your midsection from side to side).

3.   Alternating sensory targets on each length (e.g., on a series of 50s: swim downhill on the first 25, weightless arm on the second 25).

4.   Pumping the throttle: swim a series of 50s: 25 slow/25 faster. Make the "faster" approximate (or build toward over the series of 50s) the effort level you'll reach while swimming your race. How well can you keep your focus? Hold your form? That's how well you'll be able to stay efficient in races.

Of course they are. They just need a more customized curriculum. So what I do for these drill-resistant types is pull back on their drill work. We look for a minimum that just begins to cut the sensory groove for the needle, and we spend more time on the more conscious stroke modifications of sensory skill practice. They apply the same principles the drills teach, but they apply them directly and more quickly into the stroke.

Most everyone can learn the new sensations better, faster, and more clearly with drills. But if they're not working for you, sensory skill practice may jump-start your progress.

Stroke Eliminators and Swimming Golf: Two Tests of Your SSP

The whole point of sensory skill practice, of course, is not to make you *feel* better but to make you *swim* better, to build a more efficient stroke. And a more efficient stroke, you'll remember, is one that moves your body farther through the water so you need fewer of them to go any given distance. More work from less energy. Since fewer and longer strokes have been identified over and over as the consistent mark of the expert swimmer, the advantage is not merely theoretical. It's what earns medals for the competitive and personal satisfaction for the rest of us.

Fine. But how do you find out whether you're making any progress? Glad you asked. Our next two practice strategies measure just that.

STROKE ELIMINATORS

The first is called stroke eliminators because that's just what it is—nothing fancier than simply disciplining yourself to use fewer strokes than you usually do.

It's an effective tactic Alexander Popov has used to become one of the most efficient swimmers on earth. And it can work just as well for you—even if your numbers are understandably a little different. Popov, remember, has earned the title of being untouchable in the 50-meter freestyle, swimming's version of a flat-out sprint. Race after race, he takes exactly 33 strokes to get from one end of the pool to the other.

But to achieve that remarkably low count, he disciplines himself to do even better in practice, often forcing himself during 50-meter repeats to take an extremely stingy 24 strokes on each. By training his body to get by on those 24, the 33 he allows himself on race day (still three fewer than any of his rivals can manage, mind you) are a piece of cake.

If that nine-stroke spread doesn't seem exactly stunning, try this for yourself. Find a true Olympic-size pool (50 meters or 165 feet, not the bathtubs that turnpike motels love to trumpet as "Olympic size"). First, see how many strokes it takes you to swim a slow length. Next, see how many strokes it takes you to swim a fast length. A huge difference, isn't there? I thought so. You can start narrowing that down by doing a variation of a set Popov has perfected.

Its objective: to see how close he can get to his race speed without taking more than 24 strokes. He starts with a "slow" 50 meters (maybe 10 or more seconds slower than his 22-second race time) and on each successive repeat he goes a little faster. When he can't go any quicker and still hold 24 strokes, he drops back to "slow" and works his way back up the speed curve again, trying on each round to eke out a bit more speed and get ever closer to his race speed without ever exceeding his 24-stroke allotment.

Now, that's discipline. And it's discipline you can try too, using a variation of Popov's set. First, get an average stroke count for 25 yards (or whatever the length of your regular pool). Make it realistic, not what you need to do a single, perfect, well-rested length. Make it the count at the end of, say, the twenty-seventh length of a half-mile swim. You've been working a while, you're getting tired, and your form is probably somewhere around "serviceable."

From now on, that's the number to beat, no matter how many

lengths you swim. Take the pledge. Refuse, under pain of disgrace and dishonor, to take that many strokes for that distance again, for any reason.

Here's how it works. If you normally take 21 to 22 strokes per length, your mission now is to do all repeats in 19 to 20 strokes and not one more. Seems simple at first, doesn't it? You swim a series of ten 50-yard repeats, feeling fresh on the first few and easily holding the 19- to-20-stroke count. This stroke elimination's a breeze!

Then, on the second length of the fourth repeat, you head nonchalantly down the pool, take your twentieth stroke, and uh-oh. How come the wall is still five yards away?

And what can you do about it? You've sworn not to take the twenty-first stroke, so there's only one thing to do: roll to your side and kick to the wall. Hmmmmm. Evidently this stroke elimination business will take some work after all.

So as you begin your next length, and every one from now on, you become the miser of arm turnover, keenly aware of how you *spend* every stroke, making sure that you make twenty of them stretch 25 yards. The clock is forgotten. The rival in the next lane is forgotten. The only thing that matters is how you're spending what you have to spend—which is how you learn to save. Just like real life.

Repeat after me: You're working on how *well* you get there, not how *fast*. At first, a lower stroke count will slow you down. Expect that and don't worry about it. You'll also have to stretch and glide longer. That's okay too. Your old count was "normal" for so long that it will take some time for your body to adjust. Eventually, the lower, more efficient count will become your "new normal," and somehow, in all that obsession with strokes, your speed will have come back too while you weren't looking. As good teachers have always known, discipline teaches what indulgence never could.

Twenty strokes per 25-yard length is a meaningful benchmark for where the swimming wheat and chaff are separated. If your count is higher, don't slacken your stroke-eliminating efforts until you get there or below. When you can easily swim 25 yards in 20 strokes or less, try for 50 in 40 or less, then 75 yards in 60 strokes or less. But don't blindly add lengths to your repeats if it means taking more than 20 strokes per length. The only way to become a consistently efficient swimmer is to refuse to practice inefficient swimming.

When you can routinely swim 100 yards—four lengths—in 80 strokes or less (Tom Dolan, the American record holder in the 1650-yard freestyle, took 56 strokes per 100 yards while setting his mile record), you're ready to start building sets of 100-yard repeats on 15 to 30 seconds of rest. Once you can do eight to ten of those—and never take more than 80 strokes—you'll have crossed an important threshold toward swimming success. You could certainly take that stroke to a triathlon or Masters meet and show it off with pride.

So discipline yourself to count strokes nearly every length until efficiency has become habit. Then, like Popov, you can begin to trade them shrewdly for speed. Spend the fewest strokes for the most additional speed, and if you're not satisfied at the cost, try it again. Swim two or three 50-yard repeats at your lowest count. Then several more, each one a little faster, trying to reduce the "stroke cost" for each second of speed gain. Run through the cycle over and over. Get a better deal each time. Drive a hard bargain with yourself. As you master the 50-yard transaction, try it with your 100-yard repeats, which will give you a larger field on which to play the game. The game of golf. Swimming golf, that is.

SWIMMING GOLF

It's possible to get too carried away with this business of eliminating strokes when you're down to such a triumphantly tiny number of strokes that you're taking forever to get to the other end. Clever types

SSP: What Champions Gain by Swimming Slowly

When the Russian National Swim Team spent a month at the University of South Carolina training to beat the U.S. National Team, they could hardly keep any secrets from Bill Irwin. Irwin, my first real coach when I began swimming in high school, lives in Columbia, South Carolina, and swims every day at U.S.C. So he just camped out with the Russians each morning, eyes open, notepad in hand, video camera humming.

He didn't see what he expected, Irwin admitted. Impressive swimming, yes, but not grueling nor even especially fast. "The whole month they hardly ever broke a sweat," Irwin recalled. "They swam four to five hours a day, doing endless sets of easy freestyle repeats with a half-catch–up stroke." (See the hand-swapping drill on pages 91–93.)

Easy, perhaps, but exacting.

Why, Irwin asked the Russian coach, did they do all that work on this exaggerated stroke? Because, came the answer, one of world champion Alexander Popov's big advantages was his habit of always having one hand in front of his head to lengthen his body. So the coach wanted all of his freestylers to make that a habit too, and he knew it didn't come naturally. They would simply have to make it natural, "burn it into the nervous system" by running that loop over and over for hours a day until each swimmer's nervous system *owned* it. Whatever the Russian term for it may be, they devoted that entire month to practicing one form of sensory skill practice—hand swapping—with extraordinary patience. No question that it came before any hard or fast swimming.

Too bad one of the most gifted freestylers in the U.S. wasn't there to watch. On the West Coast for a Total Immersion workshop, I had a chance to watch him train for thirty minutes, knowing that he's raced with the world's best, even swimming on world-record-setting relays, but that those great swims have eluded him for the past few years. He's even talked of quitting, though still years short of his prime.

So I watched, curious, as he did a series of sprints alternating with easy recovery lengths. And what do you know? On each sprint, his body stretched out long and efficient. But on every easy length, he lapsed into sloppy form. Thinking only of physical recovery, he didn't realize his easy laps were also training his nervous system to lapse into inefficiency whenever he got tired. In his mind, the hard effort—working the physiology—was the valuable part of the workout. But his careless training of his nervous system was completely undermining the aerobic work.

His slump no longer surprises me.

can also figure out a way to cheat the stroke-eliminator system so the numbers are better but the swimming is not—say by gliding or kicking half a length after pushoff. If the real point of all these efficiency gains is swimming faster, you want to know whether that's happening. Well, just tee up for some swimming golf, the second strategy for increasing your stroke efficiency.

You don't need a club membership, and the rules are simple. For a given distance, count your strokes and add that to your time in seconds. A reasonably good swimmer can usually swim the two lengths of a 50-yard repeat in 40 strokes and 40 seconds. That's a score of 80. (Notice how conveniently the scores on 50-yard repeats approximate those on a golf round.) A "duffer" can usually aim for a score of 90, serious swimmers might be in the low 60s. Repeats of 50 yards are best because the numbers are easy to work with.

Always lower your score by reducing stroke count first and *later* by trying to swim faster. Just a few rounds should be eye-opening. You'll be amazed how quickly a bit more effort can add a lot more strokes. If those strokes don't translate into enough speed to lower your total score, you know right away how wasteful you've been. Remember, speed equals stroke rate (SR) multiplied by stroke length (SL), and just about everyone has enough SR. It's your SL that needs work. Your golf score will be an unerring measure of how well you're using SL to create speed. Fore!

We've finally finished drawing the Total Immersion learning curve. You now understand that technique, not sweat or muscle, is the foundation for the serious swimming improvement you're about to embark on. It started with finding out how your body *really* moves through the water, the quickest and most dramatic changes you can make to improve that, the drills that start those changes happening, and finally how to practice the smoother and more satisfying swimming that the drills are helping you achieve so that your new stroke becomes second nature.

Now it's time to get to the pool and start putting your new plan to work—getting fit by practicing proper technique. In chapter 8, we'll get suited up, onto the deck, and wet. It's time to start your "workouts"—the new way.

The School for Fishlike Swimming

8

Up to this point, we've focused on building a knowledge foundation that allows you to understand what constitutes good swimming and how you can swim better just by changing the shape of your "vessel." Now that you're book-smart about swimming, it's time to move our classroom to the pool and begin teaching your muscles. Over the course of six Total Immersion "swim lessons" and other guidance on how to teach yourself successfully, you will learn to swim in a completely new way that will be faster, easier, and more enjoyable. I've prepared this lesson plan as if every person who picks up this book knows nothing at all about swimming. We've found that *all* of our students, no matter how much swimming they may already have done, progress much faster by starting with the most elementary skill and progressing logically through the whole sequence of TI drills. So let's get right to it.

But First: The six lessons that follow contain exhaustively detailed instructions on how to do each drill in the TI learning sequence, complemented by illustrations of the key positions. Still, as one of our students said, "If a picture is worth a thousand words, video must be worth ten thousand words." Short of being taught face-to-face by a TI Coach, the surest way to master *all* of the essential skills is to use the companion DVD, *Freestyle Made Easy,* as your primary guide to the fine points and desired movement quality. This video has been designed as the perfect complement to the information in this chapter. For info on the video, please refer to the resources section in the back.

Starting with a "Beginner's Mind"

Next time you visit the pool, spend ten minutes watching other swimmers. What you'll see—even if you watch someone for an hour—is that every stroke looks exactly the same. Which is just how you'd look to someone watching you. Your stroke is a habit pattern, deeply embedded in your nervous system by thousands or millions of previous strokes. The phrase "practice makes perfect" gets it only partly right. "Practice makes permanent" is far truer.

As we switch from theory to practice, you're about to become your own coach and teacher. And your success will depend on practicing only the movements you'd like in your "muscle memory" and on scrupulously avoiding whatever you don't want imprinted there. "Tweaking" your present stroke will limit your progress, because the imprint of millions of previous strokes is so resistant to change. Fortunately you now have a proven alternative.

Each year we teach about 1,500 students in TI workshops. Their average stroke count at the beginning of the workshop is 21 to 22 strokes for 25 yards. A day later that average has improved to 16 to 17 strokes, or an average efficiency gain of nearly 25 percent. This degree of improvement, following several hours of instruction, is stunning for people who may have swum five or ten years with little noticeable change. The two primary reasons for such transcendent improvement are "muscle amnesia" and "martial-arts swimming." You can also create transformation by observing these two principles in your self-coaching.

Avoiding Struggle

After we videotape our students doing a length of freestyle on Saturday morning, they don't swim another length of whole-stroke freestyle until the final ten to fifteen minutes on Sunday afternoon—by which time they've spent about six hours practicing efficient swimming movements without a single "old" freestyle stroke. By then, most have replaced their old stroke with a new, improved stroke. By teaching with movements their nervous systems don't recognize as *swimming,* we've given them "muscle amnesia," a blank slate for learning new skills and bypassing old habits.

The second key to success is the "martial-arts swimming" part. Formal swimming instruction has existed for only fifty years or so, while martial arts have been taught and practiced for thousands of years, giving martial-arts masters considerably more opportunity to learn the best way to teach movement skills. Their nonnegotiable rule is: "Avoid practicing movements you cannot perform correctly." We've added our own nonnegotiable rule, which is: "Never practice struggle." Martial-arts students always start with positions and movements that seem ridiculously simple and progress through more challenging movements by small steps.

As they soon discover, movements that seem the simplest eventually reveal great complexity and can be mastered on many levels. The more patiently and mindfully they practice each step, the more flowing and effortless they become at advanced skills. We'll guide you through the same kind of progression on the way to being Fishlike.

Take a Break with "Yoga Breathing"

It's culturally ingrained for most swimmers and coaches to do everything—including skill drills—faster or with less rest. They never cease worrying about "keeping up the yardage." So let me clarify: The purpose of training is to maximize energy supply. The purpose of skill drills is to minimize energy cost. Energy conservation *always* produces greater improvement, faster. To reap all their potential benefits, you must practice drills patiently and mindfully. One proven way is to ignore the pace clock. When I'm most focused on movement quality, I never so much as glance at the clock. I'm solely interested in how easily and quietly I can slip through the water and how fluent and coordinated my movements feel.

But though I ignore the pace clock, I still want my students to get enough rest to keep their heart rate in a moderate aerobic state that allows attentive, meticulous movement. We do that by using relaxing "yoga breaths" for rest and recovery. They bring two restorative advantages: They normalize breathing, which helps keep your heart rate down. They also "center" you mentally, reducing distraction and improving concentration.

Recover During Each Lap

The technique is simple: Inhale slowly, then let your breath fall out. Relax a moment before inhaling again. You can regulate your rest easily by taking more or fewer yoga breaths before your next drill cycle or lap. While teaching, I recommend that students take at least three breaths while pausing between cycles in Sweet Spot (the built-in recovery pause in all TI freestyle drills; you'll learn this in Drills 2 and 3), as they are learning the drills. Later, they can decrease to one or two yoga breaths in Sweet Spot to make their drill rhythm more "swimming-like." Increasing the Sweet Spot pause to as many as five or seven breaths will turn any drill into a kicking exercise, which will be far more valuable than using a kickboard. If you take fewer breaths be careful not to reduce to the point where you feel rushed.

Recover at the Wall

We also use yoga breaths to rest at the wall between laps. I also recommend at least three yoga breaths between each repeat. Again, you can easily adjust your rest taken by taking more breaths. Are you feeling slightly breathless or fatigued? Just add breaths. On longer reps, say, 50s, rather than 25s, you might increase your rest interval from three breaths to perhaps five. Once you've had a chance to experiment with the yoga-breathing interval, you'll find it the simplest way to adjust your rest period as finely as you want . . . while bringing the additional dividend of improved concentration to a style of swimming that *always* benefits from more acute attention.

If you're like me, you'll soon find yourself using breaths as your recovery device in other activities. I first learned the technique when taking yoga classes and quickly realized its value for swimming. Now I use them in all manner of exercise—from governing how long I hold a stretching position to varying my yoga practice from more meditative (more breaths in each position) to more dynamic (one breath in each position) to setting rest intervals between 500- or 1000-meter repeats on my rowing machine.

Lesson One: Finding Balance and Your "Sweet Spot"

This is the "ridiculously simple" part of martial-arts swimming, at least for some athletes. You may even be tempted to skip this lesson. Don't! If you have human DNA—even if you've already swum in the Olympics—you can still improve your balance, and as it improves you'll use less energy at any speed.

If, on the other hand, every stroke you've ever taken has been a frustrating struggle, if you're toast after two laps, if you always feel as if your toenails are in danger of scraping the pool bottom, Lesson One can give you an unprecedented feeling of basically being able to *just lie there,* kicking gently, while tension and discomfort melt away. Once you have that, you'll immediately swim with far more ease, and the rest of the lessons will go much more smoothly.

HEAD FIRST?

In watching underwater video of thousands of "human swimmers" over the years, what I notice first is how completely their arms and legs are occupied with *trying not to sink.* They may think what they're doing is "stroking," but virtually none of their energy is producing propulsion. Instead, most of it goes into fighting that sinking feeling. Until you learn to balance effortlessly without your arms helping, it is simply impossible to drill or stroke efficiently. Thus, your first step is to get the water to support you without help from your arms. In "head-lead" drills, because you're unable to use your arms for support, you'll learn to balance your body entirely through proper head position and weight distribution.

FOUR SIMPLE SECRETS TO SUCCESS

1. As you practice, imagine being towed by a line attached to the top of your head. Keep your head-spine line long and straight.
2. Practice *ease.* Move as quietly and economically as you can, trying not to disturb the water. Strive for an almost Zen-like sensation of stillness.
3. Kick silently and gently with a long, straight, supple leg. Keep your feet inside your body's wake, or "shadow." If you feel slow, don't kick harder; instead, try to reduce resistance by improving your balance and alignment.
4. Most important, when practicing Lesson One for the first time, use a shallow pool section, where you can stand up at any time. When doing head-lead drills, especially if you have a weak kick, even 25 yards can be tiring. Until you can do just five or ten yards effortlessly, don't go farther. (Backyard and motel pools are often perfect for Lesson One practice!) If you feel tired or are working too hard, don't push on. Instead, stand up, take a few deep breaths, and relax before resuming.

DRILL 1: BASIC BALANCE ON YOUR BACK

Why We Do It: This is the easiest way to relax and enjoy the support of the water. You don't have to worry about breathing, so you can just

The School for Fishlike Swimming

lie there and experience balance. *Effortlessness and stability* are the key sensations of balance; learn them here then maintain in other positions.

Follow This Sequence (Kicking Gently at Each Step)

1. Hide your head. Your face should be parallel to the surface, with water wetting the top of your forehead, the bottom of your chin, and the corners of your goggles. Tuck your chin *slightly* to keep your head aligned. If other swimmers splash waves in your face, you can minimize this distraction by wearing nose-clips. Spend five to ten minutes simply getting your head position right or have a partner check the illustration and help. Patiently practice until it feels more natural and you're comfortable with the water that close. *In every subsequent drill, hide your head before doing anything else.*

2. Make a "hull shape" with your back. It's harder to balance with your shoulders back and your chest thrust forward. Round your shoulders *slightly* and shape your back like the hull of a boat. Keep your shoulders in this neutral position for all balance drills.

3. Press your "buoy." You achieve balance by "lying on your lungs," which are the most buoyant part of your body. Keeping your head hidden and your torso hull-shaped, lean on your upper back until your

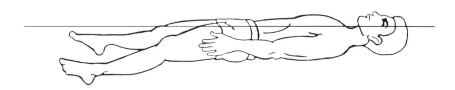

hips feel light. When you're balanced, you'll show a "dry patch of thigh" on each kick. But don't let your kick become splashy; your knees and toes should just ruffle the surface. In subsequent drills, "lie on your lungs" in the same way.

4. *Just lie there.* The true test of balance is being able to *do nothing* with your arms. If you need to brace yourself or scull with them, you aren't balanced. When you are really supported by the water, you can use your arms just to help shape yourself into a torpedo.

5. *Time to practice.* Limit repeats to 25 yards or less. As soon as you begin losing your sense of ease and relaxation, rest until you regain it.

Special Help for "Sinkers"

Athletes who are lean, densely muscled, or long-legged (and particularly those with two or more of these traits) commonly find that no amount of position adjusting allows them to achieve real comfort in the nose-up balance drills (Drills 1 through 3). These drills are important in teaching the recovery position you'll use between cycles of the "switch" drills in Lessons Three, Four, and Five, but you'll learn the sense of balance you'll use while swimming the whole stroke in nose-down positions in Drill 4 and beyond.

Rather than struggle to float those "heavy" legs, I recommend that you ask a friend or swim partner to help you as you learn balance drills ini-

CONTINUED

tially. In the Total Immersion "buddy system," your partner can tow gently from your head or shoulders in Drills 1 and 2, and from your extended hand in Drill 3. As your partner tows, put your focus entirely on relaxing; using a gentle, compact kick; slipping through the smallest "hole" in the water; and memorizing the sense of easy support you gain.

After providing some momentum, your partner can release you and continue walking backward in front, ready to resume towing if he or she sees you begin to struggle. Your partner's "draft" should make it a bit easier for you to continue independently. You focus on feeling—and kicking—the same as when you were being towed. Repeat tow-and-release several times, trying to sustain independent momentum, for just a bit longer each time. (The "buddy system" for learning balance and other skills is illustrated in detail in the *Freestyle Made Easy* DVD/video described in the appendix.)

In general, "sinkers" struggle more with the first three drills, so my advice is not to endure frustration while trying endlessly to master them. Do them expeditiously and with a degree of patience to learn as much as a reasonable effort with allow, then move on to Drill 4, Skating. This is the step where sinkers begin to understand how balance should feel. You can also use fins for solo practice, as detailed in the box at the end of this lesson.

Focus mainly on the sense of stillness produced when you can just lie there, kicking gently, and let the water do the work. Imagine being so stable that you could carry a champagne glass on your forehead. *This feeling is a hallmark of balance!* Keep it as you progress to other balance drills.

DRILL 2: FIND YOUR "SWEET SPOT"

Why We Do It: You'll swim mainly on your side and start and finish every drill on your side, but "side balance" is almost never exactly on the side. The Sweet Spot is where you'll find true equilibrium and balance and is influenced by your body type. If you're lean or densely muscled, side balance will probably be almost on your back. Finding your Sweet Spot is critical because you'll start and finish every drill here. When you master Sweet Spot, you'll drill with ease and fluency; if you don't take time to master it, you'll struggle instead.

Follow This Sequence

1. Start as in Drill 1, palms at your side and kicking gently. Remain on your back until you check your head position and feel effortlessly balanced.

2. Without moving your head, roll *just enough* for the knuckles of one hand to barely clear the water. Your goal is to find a position where one arm is dry from shoulder to knuckles and you're just as comfortable as you were on your back. If you feel any discomfort, return to your back and try again with less rotation.

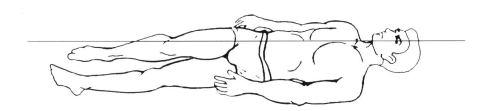

The School for Fishlike Swimming

3.   Check that your head is still positioned as in Drill 1, with the water at the corners of your goggles.

4.   Watch for signs of discomfort: lifting the head, craning the neck, arching the back, helping with the lower arm. If you feel any tension, return to your back and start over with less rotation.

5.   Once you feel at home in Sweet Spot, focus on *staying tall and slipping through a small hole in the water,* then on making stillness, quiet, and effortlessness feel natural.

6.   Repeat on your other side. You may feel more comfortable on one side than the other. I call this having a "chocolate" (better balance) and "vanilla" side. Balance improvements on your vanilla side will usually bring greater dividends. Alternate one length or minute on one side with a similar distance or time on the other side.

7.   When you begin to feel comfortable on each side, begin practicing Active Balance. Kick easily on one side for three yoga breaths, then roll gently to show the other arm for three breaths. The two key skills in Active Balance are: (1) maintain constant equilibrium as you roll, and (2) use effortless weight shifts to initiate body roll. Roll *without using your arms,* without kicking harder, and without disturbing the water. Keep your head in a steady position, with water at the corners of your goggles as you roll from side to side, as if carrying a champagne glass on your forehead.

Lesson One Practice Plan

Your most important task here is to learn the right way—patiently and mindfully—to practice all skill drills. Give yourself unlimited time to acquire effortless ease. *You are not on a schedule to advance to Lesson Two.* If you cultivate these attitudes and habits in Lesson One, your skills will be stronger and sounder at each subsequent stage:

Kicking, Fins, Drilling, and Swimming: The Whole Story

Why do I go backward when kicking and drilling? Inflexible ankles are the most common cause and the "adult-onset" swimmer is the classic case. We all lose flexibility as we age (unless you follow a dedicated stretching or yoga program), and if you didn't start swimming young you may spend twenty to forty years gradually losing ankle flexibility. Years of running usually accelerates the stiffening. If you started swimming young and continued, that's usually sufficient to maintain ankle flexibility.

The second cause is simple lack of coordination. The correct flutter-kicking action is counterintuitive. Your other kicking experiences (soccer balls, tires, your kid brother) teach you to kick with about 90 degrees of knee flexion. But an efficient flutter kick uses only about 30 degrees; the kick happens mostly from the hip flexor and quadriceps. Kids learn it fairly spontaneously; the adult-onset swimmer often has to consciously unlearn the other kicking habits in order to learn the right way.

CONTINUED

How do I fix it? Four ways have proven to work best:

VERTICAL KICKING. This won't do much for flexibility but it is effective for learning coordination. Float vertically with arms folded across your chest, mouth just above the water, as shown in the illustration. If you feel yourself sinking, tuck a pull buoy under each armpit, or hug a kickboard to your chest. Focus on keeping a long line from hip to toes as you kick. Your leg should be long and supple, never rigid. Using the muscles at the top of your thigh, move your whole leg like a pendulum. (A good exercise for the true beginner is simply to sit on the edge of the pool with your legs dangling in the water and try to move the water solidly back and forth with an almost-straight leg. Try to use ankle flexion and extension to move the water forward and back. Try "stirring" the water with one foot to develop a bit more awareness of how to *feel* the water with your feet.) Practice vertical kicking for several periods of fifteen or more seconds, resting for a similar amount of time. Then kick with the same feeling in the side position below.

TOWING. The TI "buddy system" of tow-and-release described on page 113 can also be helpful in correcting inefficient habits. The least effective (but most instinctive) response to a nonpropulsive kick is to kick *harder*. While being towed by a partner, it's much easier to focus on kicking gently; maintaining a long, supple line from hip to toes; and keeping your feet inside your torso's "shadow." After release, keep your kick as it was while being towed. Towing and Vertical Kicking are illustrated in the *Freestyle Made Easy* DVD/video.

SIDE KICKING. This can help you with both coordination and flexibility and is one more benefit to practicing TI drills. Each drill in our sequence starts and finishes in Sweet Spot. Any time you're kicking on

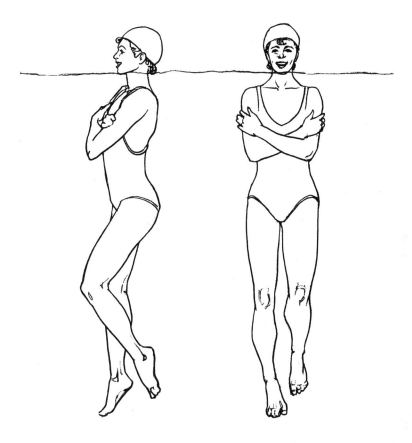

your side, you're a lot more likely to use the 30-degree flexion kick. Kicking on your stomach—as with a kickboard—makes it far more likely that you'll do the bicycling kick, because gravity encourages it. On your side, because your knees don't flex in the direction gravity is working, you're far less likely to "bicycle."

STRETCHING. This won't do anything for coordination. It *may* im-

CONTINUED

The School for Fishlike Swimming

prove the range of motion in your ankles moderately. It *won't* suddenly turn you into a fast, easy kicker.

Will fins help? The primary benefit of fins is that the blade will flex easily, compensating for the ankle that won't. In order for the kick to be propulsive, *something* has to flex, in order to move the water, similar to the pitched blades of a propellor. When your ankle refuses, it's only natural for your knee to substitute. That only makes the problem worse. First, because a right-angle knee causes your lower leg to protrude from your slipstream—turning the leg into another source of drag. That's why you don't move forward. Second, it triggers the pawing action of a runner's kick. That causes you to go *backward*. With fins on your feet—and your body on its side—pretty soon you're helping both flexibility and coordination.

Should I use fins in drills? The Sweet Spot pause in every TI drill helps your ease and coordination. *Good*. But if you have a poor kick, each time you return to Sweet Spot, your body may stop moving. *Bad*. If your body comes to halt after each cycle, you end up lurching down the pool, spending energy trying to overcome inertia rather than efficiently conserving momentum. So a reasonable kick *is* essential to efficient drill practice. And because the main point of drills is to teach you ease and economy, it really is an enormous benefit if using fins allows you to *practice* ease as you drill.

But I recommend that you try to complete Lesson One without fins. That helps to ensure that you're using the fins mainly to help conserve momentum, not to mask your balance problem. And if you do use fins while practicing drills, let them do the work. Keep your legs long and supple and relaxed. Kick as gently as possible, so the fins don't overwhelm the core-generated movement you're trying to learn.

Should I use fins while swimming? Unless your goal is to swim short distances *fast,* I advocate a non-overt kick—i.e., one you're hardly aware of. If your drills teach you balance, it should be much easier to just let your legs follow your core body. I don't encourage swimmers to use fins very often while swimming. It tends to encourage you to overkick, and you can easily lose your feel for balance, fluency, and for swimming with a seamless whole-body harmony. So . . . do use fins if they contribute dramatically to your ease while drilling. But don't be reluctant to try some drilling without them. And take the fins off when you start swimming.

- Practice each drill with no set time limit or number of repetitions in mind.
- Stay with it until it becomes effortless.
- Then continue a bit longer until you are "bored" (you can do it without mental effort).
- Only then should you progress to the next drill or skill.

Make a commitment to avoid "practicing struggle" at any stage. Any time you feel yourself losing control, stop and rest, regroup at the prior drill or skill, or do both. If you don't, you'll simply end up imprinting struggle in your muscle memory and your body will naturally revert to inefficient patterns whenever you get a bit tired.

A comprehensive series for Lesson One practice is 25 yards on your back, 25 on your right side, 25 on your left side, and 25 of Active Balance. Rest for three to five yoga breaths after each 25. As your Sweet Spot balance improves, you can do Drill 1 less often, focusing your practice on side balance and active balance. As you progress to other drills, a five- to ten-minute tune-in with your Sweet Spot before tackling more advanced drills will always be beneficial.

Lesson Two: Becoming Weightless and Slippery

After using head-lead drills in Lesson One to become effortlessly horizontal—and to free your arms from helping with balance—we can now extend a "weightless arm" to make your "vessel" more slippery. As I explained in chapter 3, when your body line becomes longer, drag is reduced, allowing you to swim faster without working harder. This lesson will give you a balanced vessel that is longer and more slippery.

THREE SIMPLE SECRETS TO SUCCESS

1. As you extend your body line from your outstretched hand to your toes, it's important to keep that line as long, straight, and sleek as possible, but don't overstretch to the point of tension. *Lengthen from the back of your body, not from the front, to stay aligned.*

2. Any time you feel uncomfortable or unbalanced—or feel the need to use your arm for support (not uncommon when doing Lesson Two for the first time)—return your extended arm to your side and rebalance in Head-Lead Sweet Spot.

3. Just as we encourage students to master Lesson One without fins, we also encourage them to feel free to use fins to increase their ease in Lesson Two. If you are balanced but still have to kick too hard, fins can help reduce fatigue and save energy for refinement. Developing a stronger kick is unimportant; a more economical movement style is all-important.

DRILL 3: HAND-LEAD SWEET SPOT—LENGTHEN YOUR "VESSEL"

Why We Do It: To experience how balance feels with an arm extended and to imprint your most *slippery* body position. Hand-Lead Sweet Spot is also the position in which you'll start and finish every drill. Finally, it's one of the two best positions for practicing flutter kick. (Skating Position—Drill 4—is the other.)

Follow This Sequence

1. Start as in Drill 1, balanced on your back, kicking gently. Is the water at the corners of your goggles? Do you feel effortlessly supported? (Take all the time you need to feel this.) Then roll just enough to show one arm. Do you still feel comfortable? Do you have a long, clean head-spine line? Is your top arm dry from shoulder to knuckles? If not, return to your back and start over. If yes, then . . .

2. "Sneak" your lower arm to full extension. *Your hand should be an inch or two below the surface.* Your palm can be up, down, or sideways. Your arm should feel as if it's just floating forward.

3. Next, make yourself needlelike. Once your arm is extended and weightless, check the gap between the back of your head and your shoulder. Narrow the gap if possible, *but avoid strain or discomfort.* Finally,

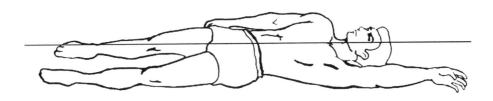

The School for Fishlike Swimming

make sure your head is aligned with your spine, that water is at the corners of both goggles, and that your top arm lies easily on your side with a dry strip of skin from shoulder to knuckles.

4. Practice until you could glide blissfully in this position on either side indefinitely. Take the time to make your "vanilla" side feel as good as your "chocolate" side; patience here will pay big dividends later.

How To Practice: Once you feel "bliss" on either side, practice 1-length repeats (resting for three or more yoga breaths between) for seven to ten minutes, alternating sides. Choose one of these focal points for each length:

1. Create a long, clean line from your extended fingertips to your toes. As you extend your arm, focus on lengthening from the *back* of your body, not the front.

2. Slip through the smallest possible hole in the water. Make sure your head slips through the same "hole" that your body is traveling through.

3. Glide silently and effortlessly. Kick gently, keeping your legs long, supple, and within the "shadow" of your body. (Use fins if this is impossible.)

4. If at any time you lose balance or comfort, put your arm back to your side and start over.

DRILL 4: BALANCE IN THE SKATING POSITION

Why We Do It: This is your first opportunity to experience balance as it should feel when you begin swimming. This is also the first movement in all the Switch drills that follow. Last, but not least, this is the first drill in which you practice the proper technique for breathing, developing good habits now that you can maintain right through to whole-stroke. Here you'll learn to breathe by rolling your body to where the air is—rather than lifting or turning your head. The act of rolling your body to breathe imprints the critical habit (when drilling) of *finishing every rolling movement in Sweet Spot.*

Follow This Sequence

1. Start as in Drill 3, kicking gently. Balance on your back and hide your head, then roll gently to show one arm, and finally extend the other arm. Allow each position to feel *great* before you move to the next.

2. After "sneaking" your arm up, pause to check: Is the water still at the corners of both goggles? Do you feel like a long, balanced needle slipping through a small hole? Then . . .

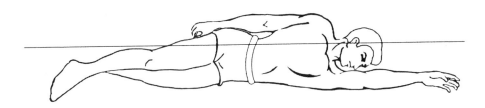

3. Swivel your head and look directly at the bottom, rolling to your side as you do. After you look down, pause and check: Are you looking directly down? Are you balanced on your side with your shoulder pointing directly up? Is your extended hand below your head? *(Put it deeper than you think you should!)* Do you feel great balance—even a downhill gliding sensation?

4. Stay for a comfortable interval, then roll *all the way back to where you started.* When teaching, we always instruct our students to roll *past* their Sweet Spot in order to breathe comfortably. If you feel unbalanced or uncomfortable after you roll up to breathe, you haven't rolled far enough.

5. Regroup in Sweet Spot for at least three yoga breaths before rolling nose-down again; avoid feeling breathless or rushed.

Lesson Two Practice Plan

Let's review what you've learned so far: Balance and head-spine alignment. How to make yourself more slippery. How balance should feel when you begin swimming. How to breathe while rolling your needle shape to where the air is. These insights will *all* be of extraordinary value in making you a more Fishlike swimmer, so you should make extensive use of Lesson Two drills in refining your stroke, even after it has become quite efficient. Take time now to patiently polish all the fine points.

As with Lesson One, there's a simple 100-yard sequence for practicing Lesson Two skills: 50 yards in the nose-up position (25 on your right side, 25 on your left) plus 50 yards in the Skating Position (25 right, 25 left). Rest for three or more "yoga" breaths after each length and practice for seven to ten minutes. Choose a focal point for each length. For the nose-up position, choose from among those mentioned for Drill 3. For the Skating Position, choose from among the following:

1. Head Position. Aligned with your spine at all times. Water at the corners of your goggles while looking up. Nose pointed directly at the bottom while looking down with your head positioned so water can easily flow over the back. Head tucked against the extended arm as you roll from one position to the other.

2. Balance. Particularly when nose-down, focus on feeling completely supported by the water, almost as if you're sliding downhill. To get this, make sure your head is hidden, that your hand is below your head, and that you lean on your lungs.

3. *Really* balanced. You'll know you've reached this state when you can glide effortlessly—almost lazily—watching pool tiles slide by underneath you.

4. Slippery. We call this the Skating Position because the sensation should be of using the extended side of your body—from fingertips to toes—as if it were a skate blade. Being able to balance right on your side—shoulder pointed straight up—is the most slippery position you can achieve in the water. Enhance this by slipping your

The School for Fishlike Swimming

body through the smallest possible space in the water, to minimize form drag on body surfaces.

5. Breathing. Maintain your needle shape as you swivel and roll nose-down to the Skating Position—and particularly as you roll "too far" when you swivel back to Sweet Spot to breathe.

Lesson Three:
Tapping Effortless Power From Your Kinetic Chain

The first two lessons have taught you balance and slippery body positions. In Lesson Three, you'll learn to use rotation of your balanced and slippery core body to generate effortless power for propulsion. Lesson Three also introduces you to the first of our three Switch drill sequences. These will be the most dynamic and powerful movements you have yet practiced.

DRILL 5: UNDERSKATE

Why We Do It: You learned the most valuable form of balance in the Skating Position. That position becomes the basis for other ways of practicing balance that bring a different dynamic to your balance practice. This drill is also a rehearsal for Drill 6: UnderSwitch. Finally, it reinforces the key skills of staying on your side as you swim and of breathing by rolling a balanced, aligned, slippery body to the air.

Follow This Sequence

1. Begin as in Drill 4, moving patiently through all four positions or movements practiced previously, kicking silently and gently as you do: Balance on your back; then rotate slightly to Sweet Spot, showing an arm, then sneak your other arm to full extension; and finally arrive in the Skating Position.

2. After you look down, pause and check: Are you looking down with your head hidden and aligned? Is your extended hand below your head? Do you feel great balance—even a downhill gliding sensation?

3. If so, then sneak the trailing hand forward *under water* (wipe it across your belly and past your jaw) until you *see* the hand right under your nose. Check that you're still on your side with your shoulders stacked, then slide the hand back to your side. Finish by rolling your needle shape *past* your Sweet Spot.

4. Take at least three yoga breaths, then repeat the sequence. You'll probably fit in three cycles in each 25 yards. Switch sides on the next length.

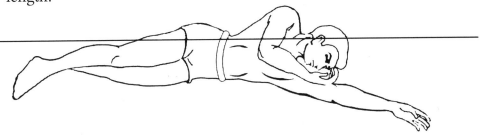

THE UNDERSKATE POSITION ALSO ILLUSTRATES SWITCH-TIMING
FOR ALL UNDERSWITCH DRILLS.

How to Practice: Your key focal points are the same as for Drill 4, but with added emphasis on remaining *on your side* as you bring your hand to your face and on slipping through the smallest hole in the water as you do it. Practice UnderSkate by itself, alternating sides. Or practice it in a series with Lesson Two drills: 50 yards each (25 right, 25 left) of Drills 2, 3, 4, and 5. Some athletes can master this drill after no more than ten minutes of practice. If you feel you've got it, move on. If not, spend as much time as you need because the skills learned in Under-Skate are key to every drill that follows.

DRILL 6: UNDERSWITCH

Why We Do It: This is the first drill to tap the power of the kinetic chain by teaching you how to link an armstroke to core-body rotation for effortless propulsion. It also simplifies the learning process for learning the front-quadrant stroke timing that keeps your body line long, by giving you a visual cue for when to make the switch.

Follow This Sequence

1. After the movements of UnderSkate seem natural (almost a "no-brainer"), move to the full drill. Start as in Drill 5, but when you see your hand under your nose, keep moving it forward to full extension as you roll (switch) *past* Sweet Spot on the other side.

2. Take at least three yoga breaths (relax, normalize your breathing, and get your bearings) as you check your balance and make sure that you *are* in Sweet Spot again. Then, swivel to the Skating Position (nose down and shoulders stacked) . . . pause . . . and repeat in the other direction.

New Moves

3. The basic movements are simple, but the opportunities for refinement are many. Practice these focal points, one at a time:

- Be patient. Don't switch until you see your hand under your nose.
- Switch by using the extended hand to "hold on to your place in the water," as you roll past it.
- Finish the switch by rolling *past* your Sweet Spot.
- Another way to reinforce this is to switch as if you were planning to breathe with your belly button. After you see your hand, take your belly button to the air; your head just goes along for the ride.
- Stay connected as you switch: When you see your hand, move arm, head, and torso as a unit.
- Stay slippery: Switch through the smallest possible hole in the water.
- Focus on doing the drill as *quietly* as possible. This will help you do any drill more fluently and economically.
- Final step: Pause your kick at the moment you see your hand and switch. Resume gentle kicking once you're back in Sweet Spot.

DRILL 7: DOUBLE UNDERSWITCH

Why We Do It: Switch drills teach powerful, coordinated, effortless movement of the core body. Multiswitch (two or more switches) drills introduce swimming rhythms (steady, rhythmic core-body rotation) to these movements but retain pauses in Sweet Spot, to allow time to regroup, evaluate your practice, and make fine adjustments.

The School for Fishlike Swimming

Follow This Sequence

1. Start as in Drill 6 but you'll do *two* switches before pausing in Sweet Spot again.

2. After you roll to the Skating Position, pause to check your balance. Lean in to feel the support of the water, then sneak your hand forward.

3. Wait to see your hand before both switches. Keep your head "hidden" and look directly at the bottom through both switches.

4. Finish in Sweet Spot and breathe three times before rolling to nose-down again.

5. Start the next length on your other side: Look down . . . see your hand . . . Switch . . . glide a moment . . . see your hand . . . Switch . . . Breathe in your Sweet Spot.

6. Practice on both right and left sides until you feel yourself gliding effortlessly in balance . . . and until your Switch timing is consistent.

DRILL 8: TRIPLE UNDERSWITCH

Why We Do It: This drill will give you even more space to make yourself more Fishlike and learn the feel of a swimming rhythm.

Follow This Sequence

Just add one switch to the previous drill. Use the extra rhythm time to feel all of the following:

Let Go of Your Kick:
How to Make It Economical and Relaxed

Most adult swimmers kick too much, not because they want to but because they feel their legs sinking. This kicking is not only nonpropulsive and energy-wasting, it also wrecks your rhythm and any chance of achieving fluency. The ideal kick for most people is one that is nonovert and nearly effortless. Your drills are the perfect device for helping you replace an energy-wasting kick with an economical kick, called a two-beat kick (for two kicks in each stroke cycle).

The only overt kicking that should happen as you drill is a gentle kick in Sweet Spot to maintain momentum between drill cycles. But when your body rotation is providing momentum, let your legs take a rest. You can train them for this by using Switch drills to learn the timing of the two-beat kick. This kick does a wonderfully efficient job of helping the body roll from side to side, which generates ample power for propulsion. You can swim with this kick virtually all day without tiring.

The learning process is fairly simple. Whenever you do any of the Switch drills, stop kicking as you make the switch. Try to glide in balance without a kick for a few moments in Sweet Spot, then resume gentle, steady kicking. Keep kicking easily as you swivel to the nose-down position, but as your hand slices forward to initiate the switch, pause your kick again and let your body glide forward on the momentum from your weight shift and body rotation. After you rebalance in Sweet Spot, pick up the kick again.

It's the same with the multiswitch drills. As in the single-switch drills,

CONTINUED

The School for Fishlike Swimming

maintain a gentle kick while in Sweet Spot and when you swivel to the Skating Position, but once your hand slices in on the first switch, let your legs pause. They won't actually remain motionless. Instead, one leg should beat down as each hand enters the water. As your right hand enters, your left leg kicks; as your left hand enters, your right leg kicks.

Don't use too many brain cells *trying* to coordinate this. Instead, focus on letting the legs do what comes naturally when you just pause the steady kick you'd been using prior to the switch. Your arms and legs already are well acquainted with moving in a counterbalancing fashion. Running or walking, they do the same: Right arm and left leg swing forward together, then left arm and right leg.

- Keep your head hidden. Water should flow over the back of your head during all three switches.

- Keep your timing consistent. Switch at the exact moment you see your hand under your nose.

- Extend both hands fully, front and back, then glide *just a moment* before recovering for the next switch.

- During your glide, feel yourself just lying there supported by the water. *That's* the feeling of great balance.

- Maintain a focus on *piercing* the water, particularly while sneaking your arm and switching.

- When all of that begins to feel somewhat natural, see if you can pause your kick during the three switches. . . . Pick it up again in Sweet Spot.

- Finally, reduce the glide between switches. Roll your body a bit less during the three switches, to increase rhythm.

Lesson Three Practice Plan

The movements and coordination were relatively simple in the first two lessons. Lesson Three involves more complex movements, though we've presented them in a way designed to ease your learning curve. More complexity brings more opportunity for confusion. Simplify by doing two things: (1) Allow more practice time for Lesson Three before advancing to Lesson Four; and (2) spend a bit more time on focused practice of each of the Lesson Three drills by themselves before combining them in the sequences suggested below.

Here are some suggested sequences (always warm up with at least ten minutes refresher practice of Drills 2, 3, and 4).

200-YARD REPEATS
- 50 yards each (25 right, 25 left) of Drills 2, 3, 4, and 5.

100-YARD REPEATS
- 25 UnderSkate on your right side, 25 UnderSwitch, 25 UnderSkate left, 25 UnderSwitch.

150-YARD REPEATS

- 50 UnderSkate (25 right, 25 left), 50 UnderSwitch, 50 Double UnderSwitch (25 balance on right, 25 on left).
- 25 UnderSkate right, 25 UnderSwitch, 25 Double Under-Switch right, 25 UnderSkate left, 25 UnderSwitch, 25 Double UnderSwitch left.

Until you have put in a cumulative total of several hours practice in Lesson Three drills, rest for at least three yoga breaths after each length. Similarly, take three yoga breaths in your Sweet Spot between cycles of each drill.

Lesson Four: Mastering a Compact, Relaxed Recovery

Having mastered Lesson Three, you should now have experienced two important elements of Fishlike Swimming: First, how to generate effortless propulsion by using your hand to simply hold on to a spot in the water while dynamic body roll takes you past that spot. Second, how to keep your body line long and to "lie on your lungs" while doing that rhythmically. Our next step will give you an even stronger sense of balance and start imprinting the muscle memory for a compact, relaxed recovery. Having painstakingly developed a balanced, aligned foundation for stroking, we don't want to let an arm-swinging recovery upset that. This lesson teaches you an energy-saving, alignment-preserving, drag-reducing recovery.

DRILL 9: ZIPPERSKATE

Why We Do It: We used UnderSkate (Drill 5) as kinesthetic rehearsal for UnderSwitch (Drill 6) and to practice a slightly more dynamic form of balance. ZipperSkate will prepare you for ZipperSwitch in the same way. But it can be even more valuable in preparing you for whole-stroke swimming because it's the ideal way to gain the most powerful sense of how to *"lie on your lungs."* Once you feel that *in your bones,* you'll know how to have a truly relaxed, unhurried stroke.

Follow This Sequence

1. Begin as in Drill 5. When you arrive at the Skating Position, rather than recover under water, drag your hand slowly along your side (as if pulling up a zipper). Keep your hand under the surface, as shown in the illustration.

2. Lead with your elbow for as long as possible, with your hand trailing until elbow and hand are alongside your ear. (Tip: It can be ex-

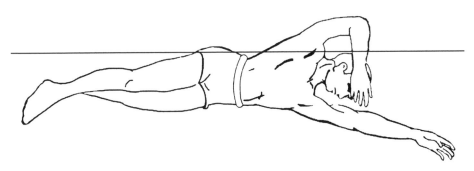

**THE ZIPPERSKATE POSITION ALSO ILLUSTRATES SWITCH-TIMING
FOR ALL ZIPPERSWITCH DRILLS.**

The School for Fishlike Swimming

tremely helpful to practice this movement while lying on your side on the pool deck or on your floor at home.)

3. Once your arm is in the "shark-fin" position, briefly check that your shoulders are still stacked, then slide your hand back down. Finish by rolling your needle shape *all the way back to Sweet Spot.* Take three yoga breaths, then repeat.

How to Practice: Over time this will probably be your most valuable balance drill and the one you should practice most often. It will give you a clear picture of: (1) how well you've mastered balance; (2) where your supporting "buoy" is; and (3) how to use that awareness to steadily improve your balance. After you've learned the basic movements (particularly the elbow leading the hand and the hand remaining underwater), I recommend you use the practice-'til-you're-bored philosophy to fully develop your kinesthetic balance awareness and burn it into your nervous system. You could easily practice this drill nonstop for fifteen to thirty minutes once a week for the next month or two and learn valuable lessons on every lap. Here are a few focal points:

1. Are you stable or do you immediately begin to sink as your arm comes forward? If you begin to sink right away, make sure you keep your weight forward and the extended arm below your head. Your goal—if you sink—is to sink in a horizontal position with your armpit at the same level as your hips and feet. This is enormously valuable to learning equilibrium. If you're a sinker, bring your hand to your shoulder and *immediately* slide it back to your side.

2. If your body position remains fairly stable as you draw your arm forward, "skate" for a few seconds with your elbow motionless above your shoulder. The weight of your arm in the air should give you a clear sense of how to balance by "lying on your lungs." If you feel balanced while doing this, practice doing the recovery super slowly. This is the nearest sensation thus far of how you'd like to feel once you begin whole-stroke swimming.

3. Focus on sensing the water resistance against your hand on recovery. Don't fight it. Instead, yield to the resistance by softening your hand and arm. How compact and gentle can you make that recovery action?

4. If you're in the "sinkers" group on this drill, fins will allow you to sense the stable support a balanced swimmer feels when doing this drill.

DRILL 10: ZIPPERSWITCH

Why We Do It: The compact, relaxed, unhurried recovery you are learning will be an important key to effectively linking your arm-stroke to the power of core-body rotation. This drill will also teach you the front-quadrant timing that keeps your body line long throughout the stroke cycle. The purposeful exaggeration on this drill is to slice your hand in alongside your ear, before slicing it forward underwater. This corrects the nearly universal tendency to overreach on the recovery.

Follow This Sequence

1. Begin as in Drill 9. Move deliberately from Sweet Spot to the Skating Position, then check that you are balanced—feeling great support—with your extended hand below your head.

2. Do a "Zipper" recovery with your hand under water, elbow leading as far forward as possible. Feel water resistance on your hand but don't fight it. Soften your arm and hand and keep them close to shoulder and ear.

3. As soon as your hand catches up to the elbow, slice it *in and forward* as you switch and roll to Sweet Spot on the other side.

4. Relax and glide in Sweet Spot for as long as you want (three yoga breaths), then repeat in the other direction. As you practice, emphasize the following:

- A compact and unhurried recovery. Continue to focus on switching through the smallest possible space, but that space is now *above and below* the surface.
- Hand entry that is exaggeratedly early and close to your head. Drive your hand into the water alongside your ear to overcorrect the tendency to overreach.
- Practice *silently*, taking all the time you need to feel *in your bones* the right moment in your recovery to make the switch.
- Continue to feel "connected" to your core body as you switch.

DRILL 11: DOUBLE ZIPPERSWITCH

Why We Do It: As in Double UnderSwitch, Double Zipper introduces swimming rhythms to the movements you've just learned. You're coming ever closer to actual swimming.

Follow This Sequence

Start as in ZipperSwitch, but do two switches before pausing in Sweet Spot again.

1. After you roll to the Skating Position, check your balance. Feel the water supporting you, then draw your hand forward. Feel the water resisting your hand at all times.

2. Switch when your hand is alongside your ear.

3. Keep your head "hidden" and look directly at the bottom through both switches.

4. Finish in Sweet Spot and take three breaths before rolling nose-down again.

5. Start the next length on your other side.

DRILL 12: TRIPLE ZIPPERSWITCH

Why We Do It: We're right on the verge of whole-stroke swimming. Doing more ZipperSwitches primes you to transition from skillful drilling to beautiful swimming.

The School for Fishlike Swimming

Follow This Sequence

1. When you feel good balance and timing and have an unhurried, relaxed recovery, progress to Triple Zipper. Focus on the same points as in Triple Under: head hidden, steady unhurried core-body rhythm, consistent "switch" timing. Here are some specific instructions you can give:

- *Hide your head* . . . Water should flow over the back of your head much of the time . . . Look straight down and watch yourself slide effortlessly past tiles on the pool bottom.
- *Keep a low profile* . . . *Hug* the surface, as if you were swimming under a very low ceiling.
- *Pierce the water* . . . Slip through the smallest possible space both above and below the surface.
- *Soften your arms and hands* . . . Feel the water resist your hand but try to recover without splash or turbulence.
- *Feel the complete support of the water* and use it to bring your hand forward as slowly as you can.
- *And finally, drill without making a sound.*

Lesson Four Practice Plan

The transition from drilling to swimming starts here. Lesson Four teaches you movements and coordination almost exactly the same as you'll use in fluent swimming. I'd suggest you don't divide your time equally among all three drills in this lesson. As suggested, spend lots of time practicing ZipperSkate to develop the great balance sense that will make you successful in the drills that follow. Spend just enough time practicing ZipperSwitch to master the switch timing. As your skills develop, spend more of your time with Triple Zipper because it teaches a range of valuable lessons and can do more than any other drill to make you a truly economical swimmer—able to practically float through a swim of any distance without even breathing hard. Here are some suggested sequences:

100-YARD REPEATS
- 25 ZipperSkate on your right side, 25 ZipperSwitch, 25 ZipperSkate left, 25 ZipperSwitch.
- 25 UnderSwitch, 25 Triple Under, 25 ZipperSwitch, 25 Triple Zipper.

150-YARD REPEATS
- 50 yards each (25 right, 25 left) of Drills 3, 4, and 9.
- 50 ZipperSkate (25 right, 25 left), 50 ZipperSwitch, 50 Multi-Zipper.
- 25 ZipperSkate right, 25 ZipperSwitch, 25 Triple Zipper, 25 ZipperSkate left, 25 ZipperSwitch, 25 Triple Zipper.

EXTRA PRACTICE: MORE ZIPPERSWITCHES

You greatly enhance your ease and flow with long, concentrated sessions of nothing but patient repetition of Triple Zipper. Do mainly 25-yard reps, resting between each for three to five yoga breaths. Referring to the menu of focal points for Drill 13, choose just one focal point for each repetition. Keep focusing on that aspect of the experience until you feel it becoming "grooved" into your movement pattern. As your movements become more relaxed and flowing, *do more switches*—as many as five or six—before returning to the Sweet Spot. But don't turn it into a personal breath-holding contest. Truly efficient swimmers find they can do effortless, unhurried ZipperSwitches for nearly 25 yards because they are so economical they use little oxygen to do a full pool length.

Lesson Five: Meet Your New Stroke

Lesson Five, though simple to master, will teach you precisely how your stroke will feel for the rest of your life. For some, Drills 12 and 13 *are* their form of "swimming," at least for a while. The great value of Lesson Five, particularly Drills 12 and 13 is that it gives almost anyone, even someone in the very early learning stages, an easy way to practice Fishlike Swimming.

DRILL 14: OVERSWITCH

Why We Do It: Our final step is a drill that teaches you how your new "Fishlike" stroke will feel. In fact, you'll *be* swimming with your new stroke between pauses in your Sweet Spot. This drill reinforces the timing you began imprinting with Under- and ZipperSwitch. That timing helps you swim *taller.* It also allows you to practice a deft, knife-like entry . . . Both of these skills help connect your arm to effortless power from core-body rotation.

Follow This Sequence

1. This drill is a natural extension of the corresponding drill in the Zipper drill series. Start with at least one length of Triple Zipper. Make sure you're recovering with a compact, relaxed—almost lazy—recovery. On the second length, raise your recovery hand so it barely clears the water and immediately reenters. Do three or more "switches" on each cycle before going to Sweet Spot.

2. Practice with the following focal points:

- Keep your head hidden and stable. Keep watching the tiles on the pool bottom during the switches. Water should flow over the back of your head much of the time.
- Be "patient" on your switches: Wait for the recovering arm to reach your ear before you start to "pull" with your extended hand. Make the switch just before your hand enters the water.
- Put your hand into the water just in front of your goggles. Cut a hole with your fingers and slip your arm cleanly through that hole.

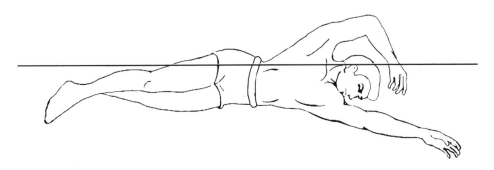

OVERSWITCH TIMING.

The School for Fishlike Swimming

- Gradually shift focus from the timing of your switches to your *core-body-rolling* rhythm.
- Once you feel body rhythm, adjust body roll to allow for fluid, rhythmic, and seamless movement with no hesitation or interruptions.

3. If you feel good and don't particularly need to breathe, add switches. Most TI students can do four to six switches with ease. The key is to sustain a relaxed, effortless, switching-and-rolling rhythm. You may find yourself able to complete a full 25 yards without pausing in Sweet Spot.

Lesson Five Practice Plan

Except for the pauses in Sweet Spot, what you'll be practicing here with multiple switches *is* swimming. Drill-based practice helps minimize the pressures or situations that might cause you to revert to your old "human-swimming" habits. Particularly in early stages, it will be helpful to "tune up" for Lesson Five practice with Lesson Four drills. Here are some suggested 150-yard sequences (continue to rest for two to three yoga breaths each 25):

150-YARD REPEATS
- 25 ZipperSkate on your right side, 25 ZipperSwitch, 25 Double Zipper right (breathing to your left), 25 ZipperSkate left, 25 ZipperSwitch, 25 Double Zipper left (breathing to your right).
- 25 ZipperSkate right, 25 Triple Zipper, 25 Triple OverSwitch, 25 ZipperSkate left, 25 Triple Zipper, 25 Triple Over.

- 50 ZipperSkate (25 right, 25 left), 25 ZipperSwitch, 25 Triple Zipper, 25 OverSwitch, 25 Triple Over.

FIND YOUR BLISS WITH TRIPLE OVERSWITCH

Concentrated practice of Triple Over can put you into a Flow state. Do 25-yard reps (resting for two to four yoga breaths) for seven to fifteen minutes. Try to do 4 to 6 switches before pausing in Sweet Spot for three yoga breaths. Here is a menu of focal points:

- *Look down* so water flows over the back of your head.

- *Lean in (swim downhill)* so your hips and legs feel light.

- *"Hug" the surface.* Take your hand out of the water for the briefest possible period; put it back in right beside your goggles.

- *"Pierce" the water.* Slip through the smallest possible space above and below the surface.

- *Soften your recovery* and bring your hand forward as slowly as you can.

- *Cut a hole with your knuckles (if wearing fistgloves®) or fingertips* and slip your entire arm through cleanly and steeply until it's below your head.

- *Lengthen your vessel.* Feel your hand just float forward with no hurry.

The School for Fishlike Swimming

- *Time your switches consistently.*

- *Move as silently as you can.*

Lesson Six: Making the Transition to Swimming

Your swimming movements are all in place now. All that remains is to take out the Sweet Spot pauses and replace them with rhythmic breathing. Your goal here is to make breathing a seamless part of your body-rolling rhythm. (A secondary goal can be to breathe smoothly on either side.) Let's review what has prepared you to do this.

1. You learned to breathe by rolling your body to the air (rather than turning your head) in all three variations of Skating. Use Skating, UnderSkate, and ZipperSkate to reinforce that habit.

2. You learned to keep your head connected and aligned as you rolled to the air in UnderSwitch and ZipperSwitch. Use those drills to reinforce this habit.

3. You developed your sense of core-body-rolling rhythms in Triple Zipper and Triple Over. Use those drills to reinforce your rhythm awareness.

4. You've worked on balance in all fourteen drills. Improved balance will allow you to breathe without driving your lead arm toward the

bottom. Focus on balance to "stay tall" as you breathe. Extensive use of fistgloves® (see chapter 13) in your practice—both drilling and swimming—can be particularly helpful in developing the "weightless arm."

We'll use Triple OverSwitch for the transition to swimming. Do a series of 25-yard repeats. Rest as much as needed (five or more yoga breaths) between reps to start each completely fresh. Start each rep with a normal (but water-piercing) pushoff and begin stroking with at least four switches before your first breath. This should not be a breath-holding effort, but a measure of how relaxed and effortless you are. The purpose of beginning with several uninterrupted switches is to establish your rhythm with core-body rotation and not with your arms. Once you feel an effortless, relaxed rhythm, you are ready to fit a breath into that rhythm with no interruption. Here's how.

1. Take your first breath simply by *rolling right to where the air is* and immediately back in the other direction.

2. Try to do that with no interruption of the rolling rhythm you established on your switches before the breath.

3. If that breath goes smoothly, do another the same way, several strokes later. If you sense a slight interruption in your rhythm, try to smooth it out on the next stroke cycle.

4. If you lose control, *go back to Sweet Spot* on the next breath and think about how to improve your breathing technique on the next 25.

The School for Fishlike Swimming

Be patient. Some swimmers will fit breathing in seamlessly right away. Others, particularly those who have the most delicate sense of balance, may need to spend weeks learning to fit in a rhythmic breath without breaking down the control and coordination they have worked so diligently in drills to develop. Here are some tips that may help:

1. A weightless arm is important. During multiswitch drills focus on having your arm float forward after entering next to your goggles. When you take your first breath, put particular focus on keeping that weightless-arm sensation. Your hand should keep inching forward while you breathe. *Fistgloves® will help!*

2. Keep the timing of every switch exactly the same. Maintain that timing as you fit in your first breath.

3. Roll as far as necessary. Old habits may be causing you to lift or turn your head. Keep everything connected and aligned as you roll your head, neck, and torso as one unit to air. Roll *all the way to the air.* If you're having difficulty getting air easily, roll *farther.*

4. Slow down. Any time you feel a loss of control, slow everything down. Be quieter and more gentle. Don't let yourself feel hurried. And finally, did I mention that *fistgloves® will help?*

PART TWO

Training Versus Trying

Finally, a Smarter Path to Fitness

Training
(and How to Get It)

"Fitness is something that happens to you while you're practicing good technique."

If the swimmers in my camps go home with little else, I want them to go home remembering that. It's the cornerstone of the whole Total Immersion program, and though I may sound repetitious with what I'm about to say, it can hardly be overstressed: 70 percent of your swim speed comes from your stroke mechanics and only 30 percent from the muscles, the heart—all the systems that power that stroke. After the second or third time I repeat it at a camp, I can see an excited idea forming in some of the athletes' eyes. "Wow! This guy tells me I don't have to be trained to be good! What a time saver!"

Alas, that's not what I meant. We're adjusting priorities, not advocating sloth. In the first place, 30 percent is nothing to walk away from. More important, however, even a brilliantly efficient stroke won't do you much good if you run out of gas halfway down the pool. Training does have its place in the Total Immersion system, and the more you know about what the training effect is, the better you'll know how to plan your own.

My definition is simple: The training effect can be summed up as the feeling of nearly limitless capacity to exercise, take deep, satisfying breaths, feel fresh throughout a workout, and go on practically forever. It's really the opposite of aging—asking ourselves (and our cells) to do *more* rather than less. That's why I didn't savor it fully until I'd begun to experience aging first. See if what happened to me sounds familiar.

I was in the best shape of my life during four years of college swimming. Rigorous daily two-hour workouts gave me the ability to tirelessly swim mile after hard mile. I had energy to burn for anything I wanted to do. But you're *supposed* to feel that way when you're twenty years old.

That must have been why I gave it up so casually, retiring from competitive swimming before I'd even turned twenty-one. Masters swimming wasn't an option back then, and without races to train for, what was the point in working out?

Sixteen sedentary years followed. The lean and hard undergraduate's body softened into the daddy-and-breadwinner's flabby frame, easily winded from just raking leaves. I wasn't happy about it, but I'd grown comfortable with my undemanding lifestyle.

Soon after my thirty-seventh birthday, the wake-up call came. Reaching into the backseat of my car for a light package, I couldn't straighten up again. Three days later, able to get out of bed for the first time, I promised myself I would return to regular swim training.

Predictably, the first months were difficult and discouraging as I struggled to overcome the accumulated effects of neglect on my muscles, heart, and lungs. A hard, four-mile training session had been a cakewalk in college. Now, I could barely struggle through one mile. But I kept at it, swimming the short, brisk lengths of intervals instead of just plowing up and down in nonstop marathon workouts, until it got easier and I could go farther.

Day by day, week by week, for the next several years, my capacity grew. In year two I could knock off 3000-yard practices as easily as the 2000-yard workouts of the year before. By the third, I had deftly upped it to 4000 yards and in the fourth, as I trained for a 5000-meter (3.1-mile) event at the World Masters Championships, I could sail through sessions of 5000 yards and more without even breathing hard. Best of all, as I turned forty, I felt much *younger* than I had ten years earlier.

So, besides an elixir for turning back the clock, what *is* the training effect? Building strength through stress. Philosopher Friedrich Nietzsche might have been thinking of the benefits we get from our workouts when he declared, "That which does not kill me makes me stronger." Stress an organism and it breaks down a little, then builds itself up slightly better than before. Give a muscle a heavier weight to lift than it's used to and it has to work harder. Ouch. Put it on a *regular program* of such work, however, and it builds itself up so it can meet that new demand easily—as long as it gets enough rest between workouts to repair and strengthen itself. It's a ratcheting process: one step back, rest, two steps forward.

The starting point for training is not the mirror, as some people looking for "good bodies" mistakenly believe, but the heart—a muscle we can develop just like any other. The amount of work your heart can do is called cardiac output—the volume of blood it can circulate in a given period of time. The goal of training is to increase cardiac output, which determines how much work your muscles can do.

Training (and How to Get It)

Cardiac output is the product of heart rate (pulse, or beats per minute [BPM]) multiplied by stroke volume (the amount of blood it can pump with each beat). Stress the heart regularly through exercise and it will grow bigger and stronger just as other muscles do. This increases stroke volume. As your heart gets better able to pump more blood with each contraction, it takes fewer contractions to do the job. So as your training takes hold, you can either do the same work (like swimming a mile) at the same speed more easily (you *feel* better), or you can work just as hard as you used to but go faster (you *do* better). The same effort that once produced a 40-minute mile may now drive you through the mile in 35 minutes. That's the choice most people make.

The other muscles, of course, also respond to training. They learn how to better extract oxygen from the blood to fuel themselves and flush out waste products, and they may increase their size.

The heart gets its training from most any workout. But most of the blood it circulates goes to the skeletal muscles doing the actual work of moving the body around the track or down the pool. Since swimming uses different muscle groups from running, for example, swim training builds you differently from running. And you can't get around that by just pouring more work on, as I'm reminded every year. If I've spent all winter prepping ambitiously for a springtime Regional or National Masters championship, by April I'll be in prime shape for swimming three miles of brisk interval repeats—the equivalent of twelve running miles. Won't even break a sweat. But on my first spring run about the same time, I'm shot after three easy miles. Plenty of cardiac output; however, the running muscles have lost the ability to use it well. But if

I persevere through that discouraging phase, within weeks I'll begin to feel stronger—much more quickly than if my cardiovascular system wasn't already in "swimming shape."

That's the value of cross-training.

That's also a lesson in specificity. For example, don't train your cycling muscles to become a better swimmer. In fact, as I mentioned in an earlier chapter, specificity goes even deeper than just narrowing most of your training to the sport you want to excel at. You even use specialized muscle groups at different times *within* that single sport, such as when you swim different strokes. If I train with freestyle sets, then race breaststroke with all I've got, I can count on my muscles starting to shut down midway through the event. The breaststroke muscles aren't in racing shape. As much swimming as I've done, they haven't been specifically trained.

And finally, even if you train exactly the right muscles every single time, they respond differently to different workout intensities. There's *aerobic* (with oxygen) training, where the muscles burn fuel to produce energy and can go on doing that for a long time. And there's *anaerobic* (without oxygen) training, which is more intense, relies on a kind of stored muscle fuel that doesn't require oxygen but that's always in limited supply, and makes you tired quickly.

Aerobic and anaerobic fitness are not only powered by different energy sources, they are used at different times. The aerobic source provides energy at moderate rates, but for a long time, as we said. This promotes endurance. The anaerobic source provides energy faster, perfect for bursts of speed, but the well goes dry quickly. It's like having two fuel tanks, one with a huge valve and one with a tiny one. The huge valve will power an equally huge eight-cylinder engine—but not for long. The tank empties quickly. The small valve may run only a meager four-cylinder engine but will keep it going all day long.

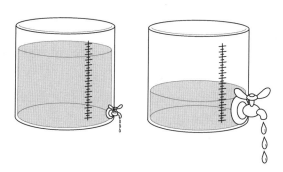

If you like to swim fast, and especially if you race, the training challenge is to make sure the anaerobic fuel tank is topped off. You could swim 10,000 aerobic yards a day and still have little but fumes in that other tank. The only way to fill it is anaerobic training.

Easy to say, not so easy to do. Anaerobic hurts! And the more anaerobic your training is, the more your lungs burn, your chest pounds, and your muscles throb. That's why it's so easy to put off over and over again. But if you want to race—as opposed to just get in shape—you can't make it purely on aerobic fitness.

The shorter the race, the more anaerobic it will be. In a race of 50 yards, which might take between 30 and 40 seconds, about 90 percent of your energy comes from the anaerobic fuel tank. But in the mile race, which usually takes between 20 and 30 minutes, more than 90 percent of the energy will come from your aerobic tank.

Conveniently, the way you should train for each event is much the same as the way you race it. Endurance training (longer sets, shorter rest, easier pace) develops the "wind" tank. Sprint training (shorter sets, longer rest, faster pace) develops the "speed" tank by making you swim fast enough and hard enough so your muscles scream for more oxygen. If they have to scream often enough, they eventually learn to extract more oxygen from the blood.

That's called higher maximal oxygen uptake (the VO_{2max} of seasoned athlete's lingo), but it's not the only way to skin the aerobic/anaerobic speed cat. The other way is—no surprise to you by now, I'm sure—a better stroke. Since 70 percent of your swim speed comes from your stroke, as I obviously never tire of saying, great stroke mechanics let you reach much higher speeds without doing much more work or using more fuel. Swim economically, minimizing drag with a sleek and balanced body, and you'll automatically be able to go faster before crossing the dreaded *anaerobic threshold*.

Still, what happens if you train one way and race another? Aren't the two really close enough to give decent results? No, they're not. I learned that myself the hard way.

In 1992, getting ready for the 5-kilometer (3.1-mile) race in the Masters World Championships, I logically used long sets on very short rest for my training. After all, a race lasting over an hour would probably draw maybe a percent or two of its energy from the anaerobic system. Why bother training it?

But I was getting antsy to do *something* with all this conditioning. So, long before the big race, I entered a local Masters meet. The 100-yard freestyle was my first event, and I mounted the block confident that since my high-volume/short-rest training sessions had me in the best shape since college, this would be a very good day.

Training (and How to Get It)

At first, it was. At the start I dove in and swam strongly through the first 50 yards. But as I came off that second turn, something was wrong. I couldn't possibly be tired! Already?

Oh yes, I could. By the time I came to the 75-yard turn, my muscles were tying up into knots and I felt as if I were wearing an overcoat instead of my Speedo. My struggle to finish that brief race gave me plenty of reason to reflect on how nice it would have been to have done at least a little speed training. I may have been in fantastic aerobic shape, but the anaerobic tank was long dry.

So What Are You Training For?

You can't make the most of your training time if you don't know why you're training in the first place. Do you want to be fit and healthy? Become smoother in the water? Build a more powerful body? Win races? They're all good reasons for getting into the pool, and they all take different kinds of preparation.

Of course, in my earliest days as a coach, influenced mainly by my own experiences as a swimmer, I knew none of that. No one else knew it either. We had a tried-and-true notion of what training sessions were supposed to accomplish: grind it out until you became a successful racer. If you could just keep the pressure on until the guy in the next lane broke, you won. So the coach's job was simple. Keep the pressure on, keep making it harder, keep increasing everyone's tolerance for misery.

The longer I worked with swimmers, though, the more I understood how complex the real training puzzle actually is, how desperately muscles need rest to improve since that's when they do their rebuilding, and how training the nervous system to swim more economically is far more useful than beating up the body anyway. Suddenly, training split into a whole range of choices anyone could fit into. You no longer had to be a college jock in your twenties to be considered "in training," and you didn't have to destroy yourself every day to get where you were going. Because you could be working toward any of the following:

BASIC FITNESS: Is your goal to simply enjoy aerobic fitness, to feel strong and healthy with plenty of energy to get through the day? You can achieve that with regular 30- to 40-minute swim workouts, three or four times a week. Unless you're gearing up for a swimming race, basic low-intensity sets will give you everything you want. And if your swimming is a break from hard training in another sport, you'll get all the muscle soothing you need from this kind of workout.

TRAINING FITNESS: Fill out a race entry form, and whether you know it or not, basic fitness is no longer enough. No matter whether you plan to eventually suit up for a casual Masters meet, tough open-water swim, or first triathlon, your training program needs to become more ambitious. Training fitness is the ability to handle difficult and demanding workouts.

Training fitness is what you have to achieve before actually getting yourself race-ready. You must prepare to prepare, laying the groundwork for your race training, not just plunging into it. Successful training is a gradual series of small adaptations instead of a sudden overload that puts you down for the count. You'll need to slowly "turn up the volume" with longer sets, longer workouts, and probably more frequent training sessions. And you're going to have to turn up the intensity too, with some of that anaerobic work I spoke of earlier in the chapter. The longer the event you're entering—from the minute or so of a creditable 100-yard freestyle to the three-hours-plus of an Olympic-distance triathlon—the more you'll ask of your body getting ready. You don't go overnight from training two hours a week to as much as two hours a day.

RACING FITNESS: Races are simply different from workouts. Most of us go all out when we race (after all, it's a *race!*), but we train at a less punishing pace.

Technically, to set the record straight, there is no such thing as "racing fitness" because it's too broad a term to have any meaning. What you need to be fit for is not just a race but a 100-yard freestyle, or 200 breaststroke or 400 individual medley. If you haven't prepared your body for how—and how hard—it will work in the specific event you're entering, it won't be up to the task.

This is an easy rule to forget. Remember my own minute of race infamy? I'd turned myself into one mean aerobic machine over months of prepping for the steady and brisk clip of a one-hour-plus open-water race of 3.1 miles (5000 meters). But several months before the big one, I dropped into that 100-yard freestyle event which should have taken me about 58 seconds. Instead, the muscle mutiny that struck barely halfway through my ultimate 60-seconds-plus ordeal was a humbling reminder that if your training doesn't at some point duplicate the oxygen demands of your race, your body will simply turn on you. It likes familiarity, not surprises.

If you compete at different distances and can't possibly specialize in all of them, just decide which one means the most to you and focus mainly on that. The rest will have to take care of themselves. Even coaches have no magic solution to this. My best race is the mile, but I can't resist a sprint now and then. So I do enough aerobic training to turn in decent mile times and squeeze in enough anaerobic work so at least my 100s aren't embarrassing.

WINNING FITNESS: "Full tanks" from building racing fitness let you finish your event and go home happy. Putting power and speed on top of that lets you finish your event and go up to the awards stand for your medal. But power and speed are achieved a little differently in swimming than they are in other sports.

That's one reason some coaches call swimming a power-limited activity. Drag increases exponentially as you speed up. Go twice as fast, the water fights you four times as hard. So you need plenty of power if you want to move quickly. But you can't just go to the weight room to build this kind of power, because it has to follow the exact pattern of your stroke—and even be at the same speed. Specificity again.

Swimmers must build this with ultrashort, ultrafast repeats so their muscles learn to throw every available fiber into the job. Since high speed equals high resistance, that's what helps the muscles build the power you'll need them to deliver in a race. It's like loading the heaviest plate on the bar in the weight room, only you get to do it in the pool.

"Ultrashort" is no figure of speech either. Sprinters do their all-out power training in lengths as short as 12 yards and seldom go more than 25, though they sometimes pile on even more drag than the water throws at them by using tubes and paddles. Longer-distance competitors build the kind of power they need just by swimming faster than their race pace. The math is not complicated. Let's say you average 1:20 per 100 meters in a 1500-meter race (equals a 20-minute finishing time). Doing 100-meter repeats in 1:10—or even 50-meter repeats in 0:35—will improve your swimming power for the 1500.

Power, of course, is not speed, as I explained earlier in this book. A powerful swimmer with lackluster efficiency will remain a powerful swimmer stuck in the middle of the pack. Remember Alexander Popov, possibly the world's greatest competitor? He wins races because his stroke stays longer than anyone else's, even at top speed. Hard enough when you're moving slowly, almost impossible as you sprint. A typical stroke rate in the mile is about 70 per minute. In the 100-meter, it can zoom to 110. And since the distance you travel with each stroke (stroke length) falls off rapidly with even small increases in the number you take per minute (stroke rate), it's easy to start spinning your wheels instead of speeding up. So don't think the most forgiving place to launch your racing career is probably something nice and short. (A race of 200 to 500 yards probably offers the best balance between necessary training preparation and a race duration that allows you to do well by practicing the smart-swimming strategies we teach in this book.) Successful sprinters invest a lot of time in patiently teaching their muscles how to move not just fast but long and smooth too. The muscles that learn best win.

No matter where you are on the training pyramid, perhaps putting down your base or already way up at the top and sharpening your power and speed, the inevitable question is, "How much can I do next?" Most athletes without a coach to hold them on course think they know the secret principle of training: "If some is good, more must be better. So I'll do as much as I can, just as soon as I can." And in this comparatively injury-free sport, they may get away with it.

But it's not the path to success. Progression—strengthening your body by gradually asking it to do more—is one of the most important fundamentals of effective training (see "Training Made Simple" page 167). But in swimming, with so much of your success coming from technical improvements instead of physical ones, it needs to be handled a little differently.

Conventional progression goes like this: Since a muscle continues to adapt only so long as it's asked to do more than it's used to, I can do all the biceps curls I want with a 10-pound weight and my muscles will get very good at that. But they won't be able to lift 15 pounds until I push them. Similarly, if you swim a 35-minute mile every day, your physiology becomes perfectly adapted to the energy requirements for that specific speed. Period. To improve in any way, you must raise the training load either by increasing the volume (swimming more than a mile) or training at higher speeds (usually by breaking the mile into shorter, faster pieces) or decreasing the rest interval between repeats.

The smart swimmer needs to know how and when to rein in progression. In the weight room progression might equal progress, but that's not always true in the water. The thrill of being able to constantly swim farther or faster must be tempered by the knowledge that, in most cases, you're probably sacrificing your form to prove that you're progressing. If that's true, you're not. Whatever you're gaining in fitness is being taken away by the cost of a less effective stroke. I can't say it often enough: To swim better than you ever thought you could, follow the method we teach in my camps and in this book. They're based on establishing efficient stroke habits as a foundation, then adding volume or intensity only as quickly as you can handle them with no loss of efficiency.

Don't be surprised if it actually takes more patience and persistence than just throwing a few more laps into the mix every workout or two, as you probably used to do. To beef up your mile swim, your challenge is to add only laps or repetitions you can do with the same efficiency (stroke count) as your best laps, usually your first few. One way is to increase a set of 10 repetitions of 100 yards to 15 repetitions, or keep the number of repetitions at 10 but increase each repeat to 150 yards, while holding the same average stroke count. Another technique is to keep the total yardage of your set the same but cut the rest between reps from 30 seconds to 15, without giving up any efficiency.

For shorter-distance swimmers, the numbers are just a little more involved. If you do 50 yards freestyle in 40 seconds and 30 strokes, can you do it in 38 seconds and 30 strokes? Or let's say your count goes up by four strokes when you speed up to 35 seconds. Can you find a way to hold that speed but have it cost you only two additional strokes? You're making bargains with the water, and you want to make sure you always win. Effective trading of strokes for speed is what made Alexander Popov the most dominant swimmer of his time, and Matt Biondi before him.

So the results are clearly worth it.

Training Made Simple

The Basic Facts of Getting Fit for Swimming or Any Other Endurance Sport

1. *Stress:* Not the kind caused by discovering a bounced check or having a run-in with your abrasive boss. In training, stress simply means a workload imposed on the body. Carefully and selectively applied, it elicits a positive response: The body grows stronger. But if the workload is too heavy, the body can't adapt. The result: injury, exhaustion, frustration.

2. *Progressive Overload:* As the body grows stronger in response to training, gains come more slowly. So we need to increase the load, as long as we do it judiciously and systematically. More frequency or more intensity—or both—stimulate the body to improve. The right training overload for your first month (or even year) of training probably will be too little to build you up more by the time the third month (or year) comes along.

3. *Specificity:* The body adapts to the specific stress imposed. So your training should be as much as possible like the activity you're preparing for in type, distance, and intensity.

4. *Consistency:* Even if you can spare as little as thirty minutes a day for training, you can still achieve reasonably good fitness by being regular about it. Physiologists tell us that we need to train at least three

to four days a week, year-round, to maintain basic fitness. (More fitness obviously takes more work.) Fitness can be easily lost in a few idle weeks, and it always takes longer to regain than it did to lose. So during a period when your training time threatens to dry up altogether, remember that even a little is far better than none at all.

5. *Progression:* The nearer you get to the top of the mountain you're trying to climb, the steeper it grows. The more you improve, the harder it becomes to keep improving at the same rate. You'll reach 90 percent of your potential with a moderate amount of effort, and beyond that even small gains will come grudgingly. When you reach that point, you're smarter to buff, not build. Polish technique. Swim smarter, not harder. The good news: The fitness ground you've already won will be relatively easy to hold.

6. *Recovery:* Work and rest are yin and yang, inseparable halves of the same equation. You need to recuperate from hard training, to *allow* your body to adapt and successfully handle harder workloads—during a set, a workout, or a training cycle. You can't push your heart rate near its maximum in a set time and again unless it recovers nearly back to its resting level between efforts. Similarly, intense workouts must be balanced with recovery workouts.

And Now for Something Completely Different
(Strokes, That Is. The Other Three, and the Good They Can Do You)

It may surprise mileage-based athletes like cyclists and runners, but swimmers can be as obsessed with distance as anybody else. And the obsession is just as bad for them.

"But I have forty-five minutes to work out, period," time-pressed athletes grumble when I warn them they'd be better off if they left their comfortable workout ruts and started using more variety. "If I try to fit in all that other stuff, I won't be able to rack up the yardage I need to stay in shape."

But they can, and their bodies know it—only their brains still need convincing. Most people can train two to three times as many muscles in the pool as they do now, in whatever time they have to spend, and get just as much conditioning from their workout.

In 45 minutes, a determined swimmer can cover 2000 to 2500 yards of freestyle. Since it's the fastest and easiest stroke, it gives the most satisfying total. Mixing in other strokes could chop that comforting number by several hundred yards, and swimmers believe as much as anyone else in the magical power of distance to measure a "good" physical workout. Farther equals fitter.

Except that the muscle you're targeting the most doesn't know that: The heart doesn't understand or care what strokes you're swimming or how many yards you write in your log. It knows only two things—how

CONTINUED

hard it has worked and for how long. So let's compare the heart-health effect of two different 20-minute workout sets.

Set #1: 1000 yards freestyle (10 repeats of 100 yards), leaving every 2 minutes. John, a fifty-six-year-old Masters swimmer, averages 1:35 for each repeat of the set and keeps his heart rate around 120.

Set #2: Later John decides to swim a 20-minute individual medley set (all four strokes), but now he can complete only eight repeats of 100 yards in the same time, since he has to increase his interval to 2 minutes 30 seconds per 100 yards (2 minutes swimming, 30 seconds rest). Once again his heart rate stays around 120 BPM.

What did he lose by dropping 20 percent of his yardage on the second set? No fitness, certainly. His heart pumped about 2,400 times in #1 and #2. It didn't care how far the body it was servicing traveled. And that would be especially true of the lower-intensity workout levels (60 percent to 75 percent of MHR [maximum heart rate]) fitness swimmers and cross-trainers stay on.

Better yet, you can actually get in better shape even as your yardage goes down. The secret is simple: variety. The heart may not care whether you're swimming one stroke or another, but your muscles care very much. Different muscle groups do the work in each of the four swimming strokes—freestyle, butterfly, breast, and back—because the strokes themselves are so different. A freestyle set helps your freestyle muscles but neglects others. Want to work the greatest amount of muscle tissue? Swim all the strokes. You'll be getting the classic double-barreled benefit of cross-training: better conditioning with less chance of injury.

7. *Cycles:* Steady, "submaximal" training is like putting money in the bank, establishing our base, our security. We write checks on that account with the demands of intensive training. Write too many and you'll soon be bankrupt, your body will rebel and simply refuse to adapt (see page 175). And the faster and harder you train, the sooner you'll get your body's "insufficient funds" notice. This applies to individual workouts as well as training cycles of months and years. Adult swimmers especially should remember: Your "careers" may be measured in quarter- or even half-centuries, enviable to be sure. If you mainly want health and happiness, steady low-stress training will keep you injury-free, physically fresh, and fit for the long haul, week in and week out, year in and year out.

No-Sweat Swimming (Why Going Slow Will Get You There Faster)

10

Let's slow down for just a minute. Despite all our talk in the last chapter about fast training, speed isn't everything when it comes to swimming well. There are times, in fact, when it's not even a very good idea and can actually do you more harm than good. The way I teach swimming, you can't become really proficient without a fair amount of slow—I prefer to call it *effective*—swimming.

Does that get your attention? It should. It's not only good news, it happens to be correct despite the fact that, as I said in the last chapter, you sometimes need to get yourself good and winded to fill up your anaerobic fuel tank if you expect to be able to take it to the limit in a race. Also, as we'll see in the next chapter, you must be willing to swim with one eye on the clock and the other on the lane lines. But in the Total Immersion system, nothing does as much for your stroke as careful, thoughtful practice at a pace that lets you stroke effectively and move efficiently. Learn to do that and speed will come more easily anyway.

That's not a popular notion in the athletic profession, and you'll have no trouble finding swim coaches who disagree with me. Too bad there's such an abundance of people convinced you must train hard all the time to improve at swimming, people who have helped establish popular training gospel. When top swimmers get written up, their prowess is inevitably credited to a litany of extraordinary sacrifices and ferocious work habits.

But coaches don't know it all. In fact, there's more and more they can learn from the work of the swim community's scientists. And one of the things they're gradually learning—though they're fighting it tooth and nail—is that easy swimming is a formidably effective training tool, even for top racers.

Take Alexander Popov—again. You don't get to be indisputably the best in the world without knowing a thing or two about technique and how to get it. So what can we make of the fact that even though Popov's best events are the shortest, fastest, most anaerobic in all of swimming, nearly 70 percent of his training yardage is below the so-called anaerobic threshold? If you said it must be because Popov knows it does him more good, you were right. He was breathing comfortably, patiently laying down tracks in his nervous system for an ultra-efficient stroke that will stand firm and propel him effectively during the precisely administered hard, fast work he also does.

Coaches can't cling to the "no pain, no gain" defense anymore either. While they have always followed the gospel that more and harder are better, the physiologists have at least gotten them to admit that adding in some *easier* produces superior results. Until recently, in swimming especially, the recovery period was the best-kept secret in training. Recovery, you'll remember from the last chapter, is when the adaptations you want—like your muscles growing stronger—actually take place. Too bad that for so many years most coaches, believing the only good time was work time, were reluctant to take a chance by taking it easy on their swimmers at regular intervals. Training policy was like the proverbial line in the sand: Can't stand the heat? Get out of the pool. Philosopher Nietzsche, coaches agreed, knew how to shape a swimmer: "That which doesn't kill you makes you stronger."

Unless it makes you exhausted and weaker. Too much hard work results in what scientists call failing adaptation syndrome. The body, seeing no glimmer of light at the end of the hard/harder/hardest tunnel, gives up on ever getting a chance to adapt and just slowly collapses. Athletes grow tired, slow, and weak . . . if they don't get sick or injured first. Some swim coaches accept this decline with their eyes open, counting on a precompetition taper to pull everything out of the fire. Beat 'em up bad, then rest the dickens out of them, and your swimmers will come through big time, eh, big guy?

And so they might. Their bodies are so grateful for finally getting a chance to catch their breaths (figuratively and literally) that they "superadapt," as the scientists say, taking a big leap forward. Unfortunately, the coaches then give all the credit to the hard work, even though it may have actually pushed the swimmers perilously close to coming apart. And as traditional coaches, they'd never admit it was the rest that finally allowed the athletes to reach their true potential.

But the scientists have been talking a little louder lately, and they've begun to get through. "Uh, Coach, wouldn't it make more sense to build your athletes up in a series of small steps? Work a little, rest a little, then work a little harder? Kind of ratchet them up from each level to the new one?" Makes more sense than drowning everybody in training, triggering a long stale period, then turning them loose with one big miraculous recovery at the end.

"And oh yes, your swimmers might enjoy it more."

No-Sweat Swimming

So coaches have grudgingly begun to accept the wisdom of training their athletes more scientifically, permitting more easy days, maybe even—*subversive thought!*—a whole week now and then of relaxed and low-key training. They grumble, mind you, over violating their dearest training commandment. Some even disdainfully call it garbage yardage. Most swimmers like it (others, the bedrock traditionalists, would still rather have Nietzsche running workouts), but many aren't benefiting as much as they could because the coaches still see a day of easy swimming as a regrettably necessary "backing off." They don't understand it's a major opportunity.

But champion Alexander Popov's coach understood this long ago. It's not just recovery, he knew, it's a way to allow aerobic adaptations you've already earned—your very conditioning—to finally happen. It's also the only good way to train your nervous system to use that conditioning in the most efficient possible way. When your heart's humming along at 130 or 140 BPM, you can work on precise skills and techniques that are impossible when it's pounding at 180. Things like stroke drills, sensory swimming, stroke-limited swims, and speed without "stroke cost." And since your body's ability to swim with maximum efficiency is far more critical than its ability to swim with maximum effort, it's clear the time spent on easy laps is probably not just as important but *more* important.

And Popov will prove to be just the tip of the iceberg when the easy-training news finally gets around. In the mid-1990s, Russian swimmers held every freestyle world record from the 50 through the 400 meters. Inevitably, the coaches of America's elite athletes got the idea too.

But cutting-edge training usually takes much longer to filter down to the self-coached adult. And if any one group of athletes needs the advice more than any other, it's triathletes. Just think: *three* sports to push yourself to exhaustion in! Plus the fanciful cross-training notion that hard work in one sport somehow qualifies as recovery from hard work in another. So they hammer in running, hammer in biking, and hammer in swimming, then wonder why they spend half their lives nursing injuries.

Grinding out run and bike miles may do some good, since those less technical sports get a bigger boost from gains in basic physical prowess. But hard swim training makes no sense at all for the average triathlete whose best bet is to never, never, never swim hard. Figure it out. In the race itself, victory always goes to the fastest biker or runner, never (never, never) to the fastest swimmer. There's even a word for triathletes who work hard during the swim leg. They're called losers. These earnest types struggle to a small lead out of the water while everybody else sits back and comfortably drafts behind them, getting pulled along. The strugglers quickly get swallowed up on the bike and finally collapse altogether on the run. Everyone who coasted through the swim goes on to ride and run to glory.

So for the multisport among you, the bottom line is this: Since your smartest move in a triathlon is to keep your heart rate at 130 to 140 bpm for the entire swim, training at anything higher is a waste of time and energy. Your take-it-easy work will pay big dividends if only you follow these two points:

1. Remember our familiar rule of 70 (performance is determined 70 percent by stroke efficiency and only 30 percent by fitness), and take advantage of it against your competition. Only a tiny fraction

of triathletes come from a competitive-swimming background. Most are former runners, who are generally very fit but who also have just rudimentary swimming skills. There's your chance, and it's a huge opportunity. Instead of working out, *practice,* using the Total Immersion methods I've covered in this book.

2. Remember too that swimming is the best way to speed up your recovery from hard work in other sports like biking and running. Dial down the swimming effort, concentrate on fine-tuning your nervous-system training instead of wasting work on your already superb aerobic machinery, and you'll bounce back fitter and faster. That in turn will make you a stronger runner and cyclist, since those sports no longer have to share scarce aerobic-adaptation resources with swimming. This is not wishful thinking or clever wordplay. Triathletes have told me over and over that it happens to them once they adjust their training to the Total Immersion method. Did I give them secret tips about running or biking? Of course not. I'm a swim coach. But I could help them in those other sports nonetheless by making them smarter swim trainers.

And what about that other competitive group, Masters swimmers (technically anyone over nineteen, but in practice mostly swimmers from thirty to ninety-plus)? They too know that better swim times come from punching up their aerobic powers. Only one problem with that. Most are forty and over, and they've had plenty of time to work on their cardiovascular conditioning. And with nature beginning to lower the ceiling just a little anyway, pushing cardiovascular conditioning any higher—unless you've just been sitting around for a long time—is unlikely. So any future personal bests will come from better stroke mechanics, not from scaling some new training heights.

What if you couldn't care less about racing in the first place? Does it really make any difference whether you try to blast from one end of the pool to the other or plan careful, measured practices? Indeed it does. And there are literally millions of people who need to know that. Considering that there are maybe 50,000 racers and somewhere between 4 million and 5 million fitness swimmers, about 99.9 percent of all swimmers have less interest in whether they're swimming fast or slow than in whether they're staying healthy and strong and having fun along the way. They need to know they can get 100 percent of the benefits and enjoyment they seek without ever breaking a sweat.

Why, even racers generally know that most of the changes in your body that transform you into an athlete occur at heart rates well below the so-called anaerobic threshold, the point where you get seriously out of breath. Your cardiac output improves more efficiently, you burn more fat, and you build more basic endurance at lower heart rates. And if that sounds like a complete list of the most important antiaging effects, that's because it is. Your muscles get stronger in the bargain.

So what's missing? Just the anaerobic training you need for racing. But if you're not going to race anyway, who needs it? You can still steadily improve because your easy aerobic training will let you maximize your efficiency more and more and more. You're less likely to suffer injuries or staleness and more apt to train consistently, since you don't need the periods of rest and recovery demanded by hard training, and you'll find it's easier to make swimming match the schedules of your everyday life.

For all but the elite among us, I say haste makes waste. Speed up your swimming improvement by slowing down your training.

Time to Get Organized—
Swimming by the Clock

Are you a pool robot? Pool robots are swimmers who just jump in and start swimming, like a big toy with fresh batteries, plodding mechanically up and down and up and down. It's the work ethic with a dash of chlorine. And even though training like this is the least effective, it's how too many of us willingly squander our training time. That's why we're about to discuss intervals—a much better way to work out.

Meantime, if the description above sounds like you, don't be embarrassed. You have plenty of company. You may also be smiling broadly because it seems to you like that last chapter on slow swimming finally justified your mind-numbing, metronomic workouts. In fact, it did no such thing. Yes, you need a certain amount of purposeful, thoughtful swimming to build skills, but endless workouts with no objective are dead-end exercise.

In the Total Immersion program we want to be sure you don't put speed before good technique, so we don't stress a lot of timed swimming early on. But staying in second gear is not the point either. To get ahead, you need a plan, you need structure, and you probably need some workouts where you push the throttle a bit harder.

You need intervals. And in this chapter, you shall have them. But not the scary, swim-'til-you-drop exercises in exhaustion most people think of when they hear the word. Total Immersion intervals are scientific swimming that make the most of your time without asking you to beat yourself up.

Although many of us probably know that hanging out on medium-throttle autopilot until our energy or time runs out won't take us far, it's how most fitness swimmers spend their time. Grab them between laps—if you can get them to stop at all—and you'll hear why: "I want to swim a mile." Like the 10K in running, it's a kind of gold-standard distance against which everyone wants to measure him- or herself.

Nobody understands this better than pool lifeguards, who know from experience that nearly every new swimmer will come up at one time or other asking, "How many laps to the mile here?" Most pools now simply post the number for all to see. Armed with that intelligence (in a 25-yard pool, by the way, the magic figure is 70.4), they begin trying to chip away at the mountain. If they can't make it nonstop right away, they'll settle for doing it piecemeal. Knock off three sets of 20, then finish up with an easy 10 or 12. The goal is inevitably to go longer and rest less until they can finally patch it all together into one nonstop triumph. They congratulate themselves, as well they might, but the glow doesn't last long. Because tomorrow, naturally, they've got to come back and swim it *faster.* Then that new challenge remains interesting for a while until the times simply level off and go nowhere. All that's apparently left then is to soldier on because "it's good for you."

That's not you? For one thing, you don't have the time to squander on that kind of distance? Well, then, maybe you're the clock-watching type who dashes into the health club at lunchtime with 40 minutes to spare. On day one, you probably peter out after 10 or 20 lengths (to coaches and competitive swimmers, by the way, a length and a lap are the same), even with a minute or two of rest between each. But you keep whittling away just as any would-be miler would, adding laps, subtracting rest, anxious to pump up that 40-minute lap score. And true enough, after a while you'll probably be able to swim the full 40 minutes without stopping, which may even add up to a mile (70 lengths). With luck, you'll even be able to pile on a couple more lengths just for good measure. But eventually you too will reach your swimming equilibrium ("terminal mediocrity," one of my campers called it) and the end of anything remotely interesting about your workouts.

That's what always comes of making the lap tally the holy grail of your swimming. You waste time fretting over how many or how fast—instead of how *right*—you are doing each one. Instead, you should be fretting about stagnation. The body gets so used to what you're doing that there's no stimulus to improve. The principles of adaptation and overload will see you through for a while in the beginning since, if you've never swum a mile, the preparation for it is an overload that does train your body. But once you've done the mile and done it again, where do you go? The world's best swimmers, the human fish who train with coaches, are always baffled by the lap swimmer's dead-end routine. "Doesn't it get boring?" they ask, since they know there's a much better way to invest their time. "Well, yes," answers the lap swimmer. "But it's good for me."

Well, it could be a lot better for you and a lot more fun too if you'd switch to intervals or, for the less technical, to what I call stopping-on-purpose-with-a-plan. You need to know how to make the clock work for you. So let's do some interval training the Total Immersion way.

Time to Get Organized

Why Is That Clock Missing a Hand?

The pace clock—that big, octagonal, white-faced moon with the sweep hand on the wall near the end of virtually every lap pool in America—is the key to your graduation from pointless swimming to smart interval training. Since swimmers measure performance in minutes and seconds, the pace clock has a minute hand and a sweep hand, but no hour hand. One minute—one sweep of the second hand around the clock face—is divided into 12 five-second intervals. The five-second intervals (:05–:10, :10–:15, etc.) are shown with both a red mark and large black numbers. The four marks (seconds) between them are black marks. Swimmers usually start their repeats on a red (five-second) mark.

The pace clock tells you nearly everything you need to know for effective interval training, whether you're coached or uncoached. Read it to find out: (1) how fast you've swum each repeat, and (2) how much rest remains before your next one.

Use it as a tool, not a tyrant. Become too absorbed with the pace clock and you'll allow it to grow into an unforgiving taskmaster. Swimmers who meticulously focus only on how fast they're swimming and never mind the efficiency price (how many strokes, how high a heart rate) are really practicing sloppy swimming. But use the clock as a valuable tool to help build up your technique, and it will make all your practices more valuable. And more fun.

Total Immersion intervals are a little different from what you may be used to. Most athletes use the "i" word to broadly describe any training that's tough, repetitive, leaves you out of breath, and gets you ready for a race. Work out, throw up, go home.

I use them differently. Yes, there are intervals that can prepare you for an all-out race. But there are dozens of others as well. The questions I get most often, and the answers you need to train the Total Immersion way, are:

1. *What Effect Can I Expect?* In Total Immersion swimming, the objective of anything we do—intervals included—is improvement of technique, whether you're learning new skills, consolidating them through practice, or testing how well you can hold on to them as you swim farther and faster.

Building endurance, increasing speed, improving your tolerance for anaerobic training, and practicing racing or pacing strategies are worthwhile secondary objectives that you should expect from your intervals. But they are *secondary.*

2. *How Many Should I Do?* Decide this way: Do enough to give yourself adequate aerobic conditioning (a set lasting at least ten to fifteen minutes—including swim and rest time—in a workout of four or five sets). But don't do so many that your technique or concentration suffers.

3. *How Far Should I Go?* Repeats can technically be any distance from 25 yards to 800 yards or more, but for stroke improvement, which is the name of our game, shorter ones are nearly always better. While longer repeats help develop endurance and pace sense, they generally under-

Time to Get Organized

mine speed and technique. Shorter repeats (generally 200 yards and less) don't have this disadvantage and can give you virtually everything you want. For greater endurance, increase the number of repeats and/or decrease the rest. For more speed, choose fewer, faster repeats and more rest.

4. *Must I Swim All-Out?* No indeed. First of all, you can measure intensity in several ways: percent of maximum heart rate, percent of maximum speed, or perceived exertion (how hard does it *feel?*). Higher intensity develops more speed and anaerobic fitness. Lower intensity is better for development of technique, for improving aerobic fitness, and for practice of pacing: learning to swim at the same speed for a long time, even as you grow more tired.

5. *How Much Rest Is Enough?* Your fitness (aerobic endurance) goes up fastest when the rest period between swims is one-half or less of the swim time, usually shown as a work:rest ratio of 2:1. Ratios of 3:1 all the way up to 10:1 are common in building endurance, and you'll see them often in swim-training books. When you do, watch out. In Total Immersion, technique and efficiency come before absolutely everything else, so be careful that your intervals are challenging enough to promote fitness, yet not so tight you have to throw away efficiency as you fight fatigue to do them.

Work:rest ratios of 1:1, 1:2, etc. (equal or more rest than work), develop speed and anaerobic fitness, since the longer rest lets you swim them much faster. A short rest interval doesn't allow enough recovery for an all-out push.

6. Are All Repeats Straight Swimming? Not at all. The variety is limitless. You can drill, drill-swim, or just swim. Use any of the four strokes you want to practice. Work on pulling and kicking with or without a pull buoy and/or kickboard. (More on use of these and other training tools in chapter 13.) Even make every interval different from the one before—descending sets, pyramids, ladders, etc. (More on this below.)

Basic Intervals: Four Good Ways to Watch the Clock

1. FIXED-REST SETS

Example: 4 × 200 yards on 60 seconds rest
Number of repetitions: 4
Distance of each rep: 200 yards
Start each repetition: 60 seconds after finishing the last one

You don't get intervals more basic than this, so it's the place to start if you're new. You're guaranteed the same amount of rest, no matter how slowly or how fast you swim. For instance, do the first 200 in 3:00 and you start the second at the 4:00 mark. If your second 200 slows to 3:20, you start the third at 4:20, holding your minute's rest no matter what.

To make it easier to keep track, most swimmers round off the rest to leave on a red mark on the clock. After a 200 at 3:17, they'd probably go again at 4:15 or 4:20, not 4:17.

2. FIXED-INTERVAL SETS

Example: 8 × 100 yards on 2:00
Number of repetitions: 8
Distance of each rep: 100 yards
Start each repetition on: 2:00 (includes swim time plus rest time)

This is fairly basic too, but it's a little tougher and more strategic than #1. You start each 100-yard repeat two minutes after starting the previous one, regardless of how much or little rest that gives you. Finish the first 100 in 1:30 and you get :30 off. Slip to a 1:35 pace on the second and your rest before you start your third repeat slips too: to :25. The only way to keep the slope from getting steeper and steeper—and each repeat from probably getting harder and harder—is to keep up, which means swimming close to the same pace on all eight. Since your tank gets lower each time, you have to figure how to parcel out the work (we explain this in our next chapter on racing) a little better each time so you end up swimming numbers one and eight at the same speed.

3. DECREASING-INTERVAL SETS

Example: 5 × 50 yards on intervals of 1:00–:55–:50–:45
Number of repetitions: 5
Distance of each rep: 50 yards
Start each repetition on: decreasing rest

Decreasing-interval sets are tougher yet than #2 because on each successive repeat, as you're growing more tired, you automatically get less rest.

Take the example above. The first interval (preceding the second repeat) is 1:00, the next is :55, and the last is :45. So if you swam each repeat in :40, you'd rest :20 before swimming the second, :15 before starting the third, :10 before the fourth, and just :05 before the fifth.

Not for sissies. But believe it or not, an accomplished repeat swimmer can actually swim slightly faster on each succeeding repeat, regaining a sliver of lost rest.

Decreasing intervals are often used by coaches to get you used to the tough challenge of holding your pace in a race, when everything in your body is beginning to say, "Hey, take it easy, will you?"

4. INCREASING-INTERVAL SETS

Example: 8 × 50 (1–4 on 1:00, 5–8 on 1:30)
Number of repetitions: 8
Distance of each rep: 50 yards
Start each repetition on: 1:00 for first half, 1:30 for second

This seems like it gives you a break, since you get :30 more rest before each repetition in the second half than in the first. But there's a catch: With that extra rest, you're supposed to swim faster. (And if you do, as we now know, you get still more rest if you're swimming fixed intervals like these.)

The increasing interval is usually used by coaches to speed you up as the set progresses, since the added rest makes the intervals easier to swim harder and faster. It's a kind of rehearsal for finishing a set (and hopefully a race) strongly.

Time to Get Organized

Interval design is limited only by a coach's creativity, and over the years many of us have gotten pretty creative. In fact, you could probably write a whole book just on the elaborate schemes that have been devised to organize your pool time with your eye on the pace clock. "Descending sets" are sets that grow faster one by one, "ladders" and "pyramids" either increase the length of each rep or increase it for half the set and then shorten it again on the other half. If that's not enough to keep track of, rest changes too, since it's usually calculated from the length of the leg you've just done. And in mixed-distance sets everything is in play, with distances and rest intervals changing and changing again.

But the four bread-and-butter interval formats above will give you the most direct route to improvement, and they don't take a waterproof calculator to keep track of. Besides, it's what you put into each length—not how elaborately your whole program is organized—that gets results.

The "starter kit" opposite uses nothing fancier than fixed-rest sets. But it will groom you for any goal from basic fitness to a race time you'll be proud of. Just make sure you follow the weekly yardage guidelines. The tougher work, for race-readiness and speed, is like a powerful medicine. You should take just the prescribed amount for best results. More is not better—and can be harmful.

Ready, Set, Repeat!

1. FITNESS INTERVALS

(60 PERCENT TO 100 PERCENT OF TOTAL TRAINING YARDAGE)

This is relatively slow, easy swimming that builds aerobic endurance. The aim is *extensive* rather than *intensive* training. Speed (or heart rate) is only 65 percent to 75 percent of your maximum for the repeat distance (i.e., if your best time for 100 yards was 1:20, you would repeat at 1:45 to 2:00 in a fitness interval set). Besides, speed is also held down by short rest periods. To work, the set should be at least 20 minutes. If you're prepping for an extremely long event (e.g., an Ironman distance swim), it can be made as long as an hour by adding more repeats.

EXAMPLES:
16–30 × 50 (10–20 seconds rest)
10–20 × 75 (10–20 seconds rest)
8–15 × 100 (10–30 seconds rest)
5–10 × 150 (15–30 seconds rest)
4–8 × 200 (15–40 seconds rest)

Remember the bedrock principle of the Total Immersion program? "Fitness is something that happens to you while you're practicing good technique." Fitness intervals are a perfect example. You can build fitness *and* efficiency at the same time simply by turning your fitness intervals into drills, drill-swims, sensory skill practice, or other skill-building technique. Try some of these typical combinations:

1. **Drill:** 16 × 50 slide & glide (or your choice) on 20 seconds rest.
2. **Drill-swim:** 12 × 75 on 20 seconds rest (50 drill, 25 swim).
3. **Sensory skill practice:** 8 × 100 on 20 seconds rest (50 swim downhill, 50 swim with a weightless arm).
4. **Stroke eliminators:** 8 × 100 on 20 seconds rest (hold at 17–18 strokes per length [s/l], assuming a "normal" s/l [strokes per length] of 19–20).
5. **Swimming golf:** 8 × 50 on 20 seconds rest. Add strokes and time for each repeat to get score for each repeat, and try to reduce your score between reps one and eight.

2. RACE READINESS INTERVALS

(0 PERCENT TO 30 PERCENT OF TOTAL TRAINING YARDAGE)

The best way to get ready for a race is to race, so on these intervals you simulate the speeds and physical stresses you'll face after the gun goes off. The usual goal is to make your cardiovascular system and skeletal muscles more able to tolerate oxygen debt. (Muscles need more than the CV system can deliver.) The Total Immersion goal goes a step further: to let you practice holding on to your efficiency at racing speeds. You do that by trying to minimize the difference in s/l between your fitness intervals and your speed intervals. Your total should not increase by more than 10 percent on speed intervals, so if you hold 18 on fitness intervals, don't take more than 20 on speed intervals.

A work:rest ratio of 1:1 should provide enough recovery to let you reach 80 percent or more of maximum speed (and heart rate) on each repeat, which is where you should do your race readiness intervals.

EXAMPLES:

(Total distance of repeats should equal 60 percent to 100 percent of race distance. Example: To prep for 1500 meters, do sets of 20–30 × 50, or 10–15 × 100.)

8–30 × 50 (30–60 seconds rest)

6–20 × 75 (45–90 seconds rest)

4–15 × 100 (60 seconds–2 minutes rest)

(Count strokes or play swimming golf on all.)

3. SPEED INTERVALS
(0 PERCENT TO 10 PERCENT OF TOTAL TRAINING YARDAGE)

These are your racing "finishing school," since they work on everything you need in a race—the anaerobic system, swimming-specific power, and your ability to stay efficient at race speeds—by letting you swim distances shorter than the race at race pace or faster. Your Total Immersion goal is to produce the most speed on the lowest possible stroke count. The work:rest ratio is 1:2 to 1:3. Sets and repeats are short and are done only once or, at most, twice a week.

Time to Get Organized

EXAMPLES:

8 × 25 (40–60 seconds rest) for 50- to 100-yard races

4–10 × 50 (90 seconds–3 minutes rest) for 100- to 200-yard races

4–8 × 75 (2–3 minutes rest) for 100- to 200-yard races

3–8 × 100 (3–5 minutes rest) for 500- to 1650-yard races

(Count strokes or play swimming golf on all.)

Swimming with the pace clock doesn't mean swimming 'til you drop. It does mean swimming smart. Anyone can dive in and just churn up and down the pool until the gas runs out. Many do, thinking speed will make them better athletes regardless of how they get it. But the price they pay in wasted time and lost efficiency is high. Intervals give you a goal instead, and a structured and purposeful way of measuring your progress along the path toward it.

And Total Immersion intervals give you the most direct path of all.

Racing.
It's Just Training with a Twist

The beloved running philosopher and cardiologist Dr. George Sheehan was once asked the difference between a jogger and a runner. His reply was a model of medical brevity: "A race entry form."

A trifle elitist, to be sure, but a clever and necessary distinction in a sport that has its own class system and a vocabulary to match. We don't. In the pool, everyone is a swimmer, period.

But that's not to say swimmers who race aren't a little different from those of us who just do our workouts week in, week out. There's something about putting your training on the line, side by side with your peers and in full view of the timers, that focuses you as nothing else can. I recommend it. And with the hundreds of all-comers Masters meets held around the country at practically any time of year, you don't have to be an especially accomplished athlete to feel good about your results when you're done.

If you've already got a meet or two behind you, you know what I mean. If you haven't—or if you'd like to do your next one better armed with a little Total Immersion strategy—please read on.

Lifelong swimmers, by the way, probably have a racing advantage over lifelong competitors in practically any other aerobic sport: Many can actually do better as adults than they did on their high school or college teams. The triumph of middle age over youth? Not at all. Nobody is suggesting that swimming repeals the laws of aging. What we are saying—again—is that so much more of your success comes from good technique instead of sheer fitness, and the Total Immersion program gives you the tools to keep improving your technique—and your times—for many years. So whether you've never raced before or are aiming to topple the personal bests of your youth, the odds of continued improvement are very high.

Don't race for medals. Not at the beginning, at least. Do race because simply entering a competition well in advance creates an anticipation that inevitably gives purpose and focus to all your training. And do race because an event swum well, an event you've given your best, is more deeply satisfying than any practice. And do race, above all else, because it's the ultimate test of how well you *have* practiced.

And as we said in chapter 9, there's no such thing as "generic" race training. You target your event, and you ready yourself specifically for it. Lots of endurance work will make you the world's worst sprinter, and vice versa. Just as in road running, you'll find event lengths to suit any personality—short and sharp speed contests to long tests of endurance and staying power. And the training mix for each is a little different. So pick your "size" (short, medium, or long), read on to find out what you need to do to prep for it, and get started.

Races? There's Small, Medium, and Large

1. SPRINTS: 50–100 YARDS/METERS

When once asked what wins sprint races, world record holder and Olympic champion Matt Biondi replied, "Four things: technique, technique, technique, and speed." It doesn't take much endurance to swim as fast as you can for twenty to ninety seconds. A deadly efficient stroke is what you need. Just make sure you can hold your stroke length when you're going as fast as you possibly can, when your heart rate is crashing through the roof, and lactic acid is flooding into your hapless and hurting muscles.

Efficiency is so critical in short races because you're probably going 20 percent to 25 percent faster in the 100 meters than the 1500, for example, and the difference in drag and the power needed to overcome it is enormous. Small inefficiencies become hugely magnified in a sprint.

But you can't overlook the need to supply enough energy and oxygen to muscles that are gulping it down for all they're worth, powering your body through this over-the-top effort. Your system also has to whisk away all that energy-sapping lactic acid as fast as your muscles produce it if they're to keep going.

All that means anaerobic training, of course, and you can't let your stroke get sloppy while pushing the practice pace.

Finally, you need the power that comes from training your neuromuscular system to fire up all available muscle motor units to overcome whatever drag your stroke efficiency hasn't eliminated. That means swimming "power sets," short reps at top effort. (See the appendix for some suggestions.)

2. MIDDLE DISTANCE: 200–400 YARDS/METERS

Sometimes called speed/endurance events because they take both, these are among the most difficult to train for. You don't get a break. Speeds are fairly close to the sprint, but you've got to hold on for up to ten times as long. It's not the higher stroke rate of the shorter sprints that will crack your technique and efficiency but the surprising amount of anaerobic work in these races, even though they're longer and slower than sprints. It's hard to stay fussy about your stroke over an entire quarter mile without enough air.

Of course, as your technique starts to come apart, the "energy cost" of holding your speed inflates even as you have less and less left with every tick of the stopwatch. So middle-distance racers need a two-pronged training strategy:

1. Long, aerobic sets for endurance—sets that will do far more good if they train the nervous system right along with the aerobic system, focusing on stroke efficiency too.

2. Race-pace swimming, to develop endurance at higher speeds and get you used to the stroke rate and anaerobic conditions that make these distances such a thorough test.

What it all comes down to is finding and holding the right pace—staying out of oxygen debt, operating aerobically for as long as you can. (The more efficient your stroke, remember, the longer you can hold on to that aerobic state of grace.) It's a hard trick to pull off unless you swim most of the race at an even pace. A blazing first half usually guarantees a painful second half. That's why the world's best middle-distance swimmers almost always swim the second half as fast as or even faster than the first. And mastering that tactic takes practice. (See the appendix for some suggestions.)

3. DISTANCE SWIMMING: 800 METERS AND UP

For the thousands of runners who turn to swimming every year to find less body-punishing workouts and who think of a two-mile footrace as barely the far side of a sprint, the comparatively short distance–horizon in swimming comes as a surprise. The 1500 meter, which may take a top contender fifteen to twenty minutes—nearly the same time as a 5K run—is the longest event most swimmers ever enter. And the marathon's time span of three to five hours, a fairly common experience for runners, is all but unheard of in swimming.

So why all the emphasis on high-yardage training? Because swim coaches believe we must not only develop endurance but also "feel for the water," which is really just another way of saying natural efficiency. And they believe it takes years of practice and millions of yards of repetition to develop this.

It doesn't. If you can accelerate the development of an efficient stroke, which is just what you're learning to do in this book, then you can drastically reduce the yardage it takes to prep for an endurance swim. Instead, you work on developing what I call efficiency endurance, the ability to keep your stroke the same whatever distance you swim. Training sets up to half again the distance of your race will do this if you use them to practice and improve your ability to keep your stroke long and efficient, lap after lap after lap.

The second reason coaches push so much high-yardage training on swimmers is to develop the "clock in the head," the instinct for swimming at just the right pace so they don't kill the race by overswimming at the beginning. Distance swimmers practice pacing endlessly, learning how to keep going at the same pace for lap after lap even as fatigue mounts. One way to shorten the learning curve is by swimming descending reps, which we mentioned in the last chapter, in which each one gets progressively faster during a long set. (See the appendix for samples.)

How to Be Ready. Really Ready

Good training doesn't necessarily guarantee a good race. The lead spots go to those who've done their homework, from deciding how much warmup they'll need to knowing how the event plays out, what to expect on every length.

If you've done the homework for a 1650-yard freestyle (the equivalent of the 1500-meter event) you can get yourself ready for most anything. Otherwise known as swimming's metric mile, it's 66 lengths of a 25-yard pool, and though it's my personal favorite, I always approach it with a love-hate attitude. Love because it's my best distance and the one in which I've always reached my highest national rankings (a couple of seconds). Hate because it promises lots of pain.

I've swum longer races that felt easier. I've *run* longer races more comfortably, even though I'm a much better swimmer than runner. A 45- to 50-minute 10K footrace doesn't seem anywhere near as long as a 1650 in the pool, which I can knock off in maybe 18 or 19 minutes. Even a 5K open-water swim, which took me 68 minutes, was easier than any 1650-yard race I've ever swum in a pool.

Perhaps it's because of the need for such fierce concentration on keeping your stroke efficient, with every lap feeling harder than the last. Perhaps it's all the flip turns that make it hard to stay aerobic as the laps mount. But whatever the reason, this race tests it all: your mental focus, the staying power of your efficiency, and the quality of your conditioning. So getting ready for it is a virtual punch list for all prerace preparation. Based on personal experience, here's how I advise leading up to and handling a 1650. If you're prepping for a shorter distance, just adapt my routine to suit.

Several days before, I begin to think about what it will feel like if I'm willing to take it to the limit and not back off in the race when the body starts imploring me to. Will this be a redline effort or something less? Redline, of course.

Come competition day I get in the mood with a long, easy, pre-event warmup—typically at least forty to forty-five minutes for a race that takes less than half as long. This does several things. First, just swimming smoothly and easily takes the nervous edge off. Second, you can use the warmup to groove your stroke into what coaches call easy speed, a relaxed, familiar rhythm, a feeling of being controlled and effortless at your projected race pace. It takes at least several minutes to get that, but I don't want to spend the first 500 of my 1650 groping around for it, so I rehearse the feeling now.

And I rehearse until it's right, maybe six or eight 100-yard repeats—nearly half the distance of the race itself—trying to hit target pace precisely on each with that buoyant feeling of easy speed. To race sixteen

Racing: Training with a Twist

identically paced 100s, you have to go a little harder on each as a new layer of fatigue settles into your muscles. The first few will feel nearly effortless, the last ones will feel like you're lifting a piano. If I can hit six or eight of these with 15 to 20 seconds of rest between, I'm more confident that once the gun goes off, I'll be able to reel off sixteen in a row, with no rest, at the same pace.

You'll probably feel better in the early stages of a distance race if you finish your warmup/rehearsal just before your heat starts. There's something to be said for going right from the warmup pool to the starting blocks, with your muscles prepared and your race rhythms all set. Done correctly, a long warmup like this right before the race gives you a net gain in the gas tank, since what you've been practicing is energy conservation.

You've also been setting that confidence-building "clock in the head," the coach's term for an unerring sense of pace. Pool racing is done one to a lane, so there's no such thing as drafting behind anyone. And you might not want to try even if you could. The 1650 is too long to try to swim someone else's race. You perform far better when you do it the way *you've* trained for it. That means having a goal time in mind and a pace plan for reaching it.

Finally it's time to race. When the gun goes off and you dive in after this kind of prep work, you'll become quite calm. From the first, your stroke feels just the way you want it to. Now's the time to be patient. For the first 400 to 500 yards (16 to 20 lengths), avoid racing. You're stalking. Keep your stroke as long as possible and your stroke rate as low as possible, and stay within striking distance of your rivals. Everything goes into efficiency, so it's indelibly imprinted onto your nervous system and the coming fatigue and racing pressures can't break it down.

Whatever you do, stay out of oxygen debt. You're excited. You may be trying to keep up. It's too easy to overswim the first part of any race and slip across the anaerobic threshold. Once you do, the only way to recover will be to slow down, and once you've slackened the pace, it's nearly impossible to push it all the way up again. Oh, eventually you'll have to go anaerobic just to hold on to your pace, but you want that to come as near the end of the race as possible. Stay aerobic for three quarters of the race, and you'll have what it takes in the tanks for the last few 100s.

Eventually, you'll be playing a cat-and-mouse game with fatigue. In a sheer act of will, you try to keep your stroke long, but as you get a little more tired your only recourse is to increase stroke rate—carefully. Do this with hip rolling, not muscle power. (Your muscles don't have that much to spare by now anyhow.) Try to dial it up just a little on each 100 to exactly offset fatigue. It's a delicate game, but if you've practiced enough, you can play it successfully.

You're up to about 1200 yards now, but who's counting? The answer is, friends are. At the end of the pool opposite the starting blocks, a card showing the lap number is shoved in front of your face just before every turn. This race takes so much concentration that it's impossible to keep track of your lap count, so a friend kneels at the end of your lane and obligingly shoves those numbered cards into the water, shouting encouragement as you turn.

You're closing in now. The last sixteen to twenty lengths, and it's time to really bear down. Begin to count. The card reads 51, you're headed into lap 52, and you're thinking, Only fourteen to go—I can bring this home.

Time to find out what you're made of. No matter how easily you

Racing: Training with a Twist

swam the beginning, no matter how intelligent your pace in the middle, your whole body will start to ache for oxygen over the last few hundred yards. Every flip turn seems like an aerobic slap in the face, since the flip turn cuts off your oxygen for a few seconds at each wall. Great. Just what you need. An open turn with your face above water would be so nice, but it costs precious fractions at each wall and you didn't come this far to throw time away now. Too bad it seems like you need the whole length to get your breath back from every turn and just when you have, you get slapped down again.

Eight lengths to go. Now six. Now just four. Each 50 gets harder, but each brings you closer to relief. Finally, you pour everything you have left into the last two lengths, thrust your hand to the touch pad, and it's over!

For a couple of minutes even hanging exhausted on the gutter will hurt, as lactic acid pools in the muscles that generated it. So push off and swim a few massaging laps of easy backstroke to wash some of it out. You're finished. You've taken your Total Immersion training into the contest and proven that even when the rest of the body falters, your muscles can go on autopilot if you've trained them well.

And for me at least, racing like this is an exercise in self-discovery. My final time interests me less than the broader revelation of how well my training has prepared me to race on this particular day. I'm more curious about testing my abilities to execute a good race plan than in what color medal I may have won. And every race I swim presents its own set of lessons, which I am always eager to apply when I return to the pool for my next practice.

Pool Tools:
Less Is More

Make no mistake about it. You can become an excellent swimmer with nothing more than your own body, a swimsuit, and some smart coaching. No accessories necessary.

But there are plenty available. Some of them are actually helpful. Kickboards may be the most familiar, followed closely by fins. Hand paddles, pull buoys, elastic tethers—all beckon with the promise of greater strength or more impressive speed. They supposedly work like weight machines of the water, letting you isolate muscles you need to work on, then bear down on them with concentrated training.

Some are beneficial. Others at least won't do you particular harm. And still others sound good but are a waste of time at best and an actual detriment to your swimming at worst. It's true that virtually everyone uses them, but this is one of those cases where most folks just have the wrong idea about what these training aids really do. So let's give them a critical analysis.

Of all the elements that make up the hard-to-define gift known as "swimming talent," the most valuable is extraordinary kinesthetic awareness—gifted swimmers just know how to work *with* the water better than anyone else to achieve less resistance and more fluid movement. But, as I've suggested, a surprising amount of what coaches call "talent" is *learnable.* "Average" swimmers can unquestionably heighten their own kinesthetic awareness, which will always produce more improvement, more quickly, than anything under the heading of "work."

The most commonly used training tools have two drawbacks: (1) they encourage you to focus on effort, rather than efficiency; and (2) they actively interfere with your ability to improve your kinesthetic awareness. Finally, for developing swimmers there is also the issue of prioritizing precious time for activities that have the largest value. TI methods help you swim better *immediately.* Buoys, boards, and paddles simply don't.

Just Say No to Kickboards

The main idea of kickboard training is to get your legs in shape for kicking *harder.* And why would you want to kick harder? (1) Because you feel your legs sinking, (2) to swim faster, or (3) to burn more calories or fat. But (1) balance—taught by TI drills—is what keeps your legs afloat. And (2) the ideal kick for fast, fluent swimming is one that harmonizes seamlessly with overall body movement. Finally, (3) as the next chapter will explain, the best way to burn calories and fat is with *easier* swimming. The truth about kickboards is they will contribute absolutely nothing to your efforts to improve your freestyle, whether you're just learning or are training for a national championship. The flutter used on a kickboard—with arms, torso, and hips rigidly locked in place—is so different from the kick you'll use when swimming that kickboard sets have zero value for developing a kick that helps your body move efficiently through the water. Ditto for "conditioning your legs."

Because your legs move so differently when kicking on a board than while swimming, the only thing a kickboard really trains you for is *kicking with a board*. If you ever planned to enter a race that involved pushing a kickboard up and down the pool, then kickboard sets would make sense; otherwise, *it's a total waste of time!* If you want your legs to be "in shape" for swimming, the relaxed kicking you do while practicing TI drills conditions your legs to do exactly what they need to do when you race: stay relaxed. You are dispensed from using a kickboard ever again.

Lose the Buoy

Pull buoys have one central drawback: They fool you into thinking you're balanced. They're so popular with thousands of swimmers because poor balance is such a common problem. So long as you have a buoy on, it supports your hips and legs. You feel better and swim faster. The problem is that using it never seems to teach you how to stay balanced *after* you use it. As soon as you remove the buoy, that sinking feeling is right back and you're no better off than before. Want to feel better *without* the buoy—permanently? Balance drills, keeping your head in line with your spine, swimming "downhill," and swimming with fistgloves® produce lasting lessons in how to stay balanced while you swim.

And as for the idea that training with a buoy strengthens your pull by overloading and isolating your arms, in fact, it does just the opposite. The artificial buoyancy of the buoy raises your body in the water; it *underloads* your arms—no training benefit at all. Moreover, using a buoy can actually hurt your stroking power, because power doesn't come from the arms; it comes from core-body rotation. Buoys are likely to inhibit your body roll, interfering with your rhythm and power. Fortunately, once you do learn balance, putting on a buoy should feel all wrong, which will soon discourage you from using one.

The sole circumstance in which there might be some value in using a buoy is this: If you are one of those extremely lean or densely muscled athletes who seems permanently balance-challenged, if you experience what feels like terminal struggle while doing balance drills, if you have a "frantic" kick, you may be able to selectively use a buoy as one way to break the cycle of struggling. Using a fairly small buoy, swim a relaxed pool length. Keep your head in line and swim as silently as you can. As you do, tune in to how it feels to be supported, to be able to glide an unhurried arm forward and swim a little "taller," to be able to *let go of your kick.* Can't feel it after one length? Do a few more 25s that way. When those sensations come, just capture and imprint them. Then remove the buoy and swim two 25s without it. Keep your head in line and swim downhill. Swim as gently and quietly as possible. You have just one goal: to get your no-buoy laps to feel as much like the buoy lap as possible. Patiently repeat this pattern for ten or fifteen minutes. As your no-buoy laps begin to feel as relaxed as the buoyed laps, add more unbuoyed 25s.

Smart Hands Are Better Than Dumb Plastic

The rap on hand paddles is pretty simple: You put them on and suddenly feel as if you can really grab the water and move it powerfully. Paddles are usually emphasized as a power tool (and the bigger the paddle, the better—or so the theory goes). You use the extra surface area to muscle the water. But unless you have a *perfect* stroke, muscling the water with paddles is mainly a good way to improve your chances of shoulder injury. And if you're lucky enough to avoid injury, once you take them off, you feel like you're trying to row with a Popsicle stick. What could be good about that?

As with pull buoys, there is one small exception. You might occasionally don small paddles for a few superslow laps with a narrow focus on how they may help your hand learn to *pierce* the water . . . or slide weightlessly forward a looong way . . . or anchor for the catch. Then remove them and, as suggested above for buoy use, try to recreate that sensation without the paddles. Unless you can subtract at least two strokes with the paddles on, they're not helping you at all.

For *intelligent* hands that can teach you to work with water like an artist, consider fistgloves®. Fistgloves have proven so indispensable as an aid to teaching TI-style swimming that we give a pair to every student at TI Weekend Workshops. We like them because they turn any swimmer into a problem solver and the solution you come up with will help you hold the water like never before.

The problem fistgloves® present is: How do you hold on to the water when you have nothing to hold on with? By squeezing the hands into a tight, latex-wrapped fist, fistgloves® turn a broad, flat surface into a rubber nub. On the first few lengths, your hands slip helplessly through the water. But gradually, you find *one molecule of water* to hold on to, partly by using your forearm for purchase, partly by simply learning to be more patient. Just by making the catch with exquisite patience and attention, you will eventually learn to get the water to resist your gloved hands *just a little bit*. With practice you can learn to do remarkable things with the slightest resistance. So much so that by continuing to stroke patiently, the gloved-swimming sensation will gradually come to feel almost "normal." After a while, you may even wonder if you're wearing a glove. Measure how much control you're gaining by counting strokes per length and playing Swimming Golf.

The real magic, of course, happens when you peel the gloves off. Suddenly, your previously ordinary-feeling hand seems *huge,* as if you had a dinner-plate-sized paddle at the end of your arm and holding on to the water turns out to be a piece of cake.

Why are fistgloves® better than paddles for teaching feel of the water? Because paddles do exactly the opposite. Swimmers figure they'll learn how it feels to have "big hands," and that once the paddles come off they'll remember the sensation they're aiming for. While the paddles are on, you do of course feel much more able to hold the water. But when the paddles come off? You feel like someone rowing with a Popsicle stick. Your hands seem dumb, ineffectual. So we sometimes call fistgloves® the "unpaddles," because after using fistgloves® your hands seem smarter, not dumber.

The simplest and best way to use fistgloves® is to wear them for the first twenty to twenty-five minutes of every practice, whatever you may be doing during that time. Every lap will help your balance and finesse. When you take them off you'll swim with far more intuition the rest of the way. Or, during a 60-minute practice, you might wear them for 20 minutes, remove them for 10, put them on again for 20 minutes and swim without them for 10.

Fins as a Learning Aid, Not for Temporary Speed

The most common use of fins I've seen is by those who want a dose of instant speed. So they put on fins and instantly can swim much faster laps. But, as with buoys and paddles, that's precisely the problem with fins. They're a temporary and artificial aid that helps you swim easier or faster while you have them on, but the effect disappears as soon as you take them off. No learning happens. *None.* Wearing fins to be faster is like wearing platform shoes to be taller.

What fins might do, when used this way, is interfere with your ability to develop a fluent, relaxed, efficient stroke into a reliable habit. Short-blade fins, in particular, are *specifically* designed to help you kick faster than you could with full-blade fins. And the faster your legs move, the faster your arms have to move to keep up. Isn't faster turn-over (i.e., higher SR) precisely what we're trying to *avoid?* Short fins were designed originally to help sprint swimmers achieve high stroke rates while swimming with fin-aided speed—and to condition a swimmer's legs for the *hard* kicking that is typical when sprinting. Again, that's precisely the kind of thing a TI swimmer wants to avoid.

There are exceptions with fins as well. As I explained in chapter 8, they can be very helpful to anyone whose rigid ankles make drill practice an ordeal. Using fins to preserve your energy and allow yourself to focus on smooth, more controlled movement is an aid to mastering skills. For the most part, even if you use fins judiciously to improve your drill practice, it's best to take them off as soon as you shift to whole-stroke swimming.

Swim Benches

Swim benches have been promoted as better, in some ways, than actually swimming in a pool. Their manufacturers promise they'll perfect your stroke and allow you to get as good a "swim" workout at home as you could going to the pool, et cetera, et cetera. The fact is that these benches *will* make your arms stronger and give you a workout of sorts, but I'm highly skeptical that they'll improve your swimming. A body moving through water and a body lying on a bench behave in entirely different ways. The biomechanics (the way muscle groups interact) and the kinesthetics (your "muscle sense") are dramatically different from bench to pool. Swim bench workouts train you best to do swim bench workouts. If you're planning to enter swim bench competition, then by all means train on one. If you must have something at home to supplement your swimming, you can get a device that sells for about 5 percent of what the least expensive swim bench costs, yet will provide 90 percent of its benefit. It's called a stretch cord.

Stretch Cords

Stretch cords are lengths of latex tubing with handles at each end and a nylon loop in the middle that can anchor to a wide variety of fixed objects. Cords have been one of my favorite training aids for over twenty years because they're the most affordable and versatile of any strength-building tool that can legitimately be recommended for swimmers. In fact, a study at the University of New Brunswick found that a daily stretch cord workout of 20 minutes (12 to 14 minutes of exercise, 6 to 8 minutes of rest) helped swimmers hang on to virtually all of their conditioning during a three-week layoff.

Stretch cords give you the same steady, fluid resistance that water does. They also let you work through a virtually endless range of motion, limited only by your joints and your workout space. If you use weights to build swimming strength, you can also use cords as a "bridge" between nonspecific strength work in the weight room and swim-specific movement in the pool. Weight training builds muscles that are most specific to the movements you use while lifting the weights. Swimming uses those muscles differently and always in a low-load situation. Stretch cord training helps translate your weight room strength to pool strength by working your muscles in swimming-specific motions, but under much higher loads than water could provide.

Finally, cords can be easily used for "prehab" exercise to correct muscle imbalances caused by swimming, and to strengthen the shoulder joint to protect against tendinitis and other injuries. In fact, physical therapists prescribe stretch cord exercises to rehab many shoulder injuries.

Swim Flumes

As I write this I'm having my basement prepared for the installation of an Endless Pool, a flume pool that circulates a water current in the front end and out the back. In an earlier edition of this book, I described concerns about how the dynamics of swimming in place while water moves past you could hurt the efficiency that Total Immersion practice is designed to build. In the last few years, with experience in an Endless Pool, I've changed my mind.

With the current set at slower speeds, the Endless Pool has proven, for a growing number of TI coaches, to be a convenient and effective place for both teaching and practicing TI drills and skills. But if you keep the current cranked up high, the resulting stroke will be just as bad for you as swimming hard all the time. The primary virtues of a flume pool with a moderate current are these:

- Because there is no "wall" and no need to interrupt your swimming and head back the other way, you quite literally have an *endless* pool. A distraction of practicing TI drills or skills in a 25-yard pool is that you often find yourself just getting into the rhythm, or tuning into the sensation you're after as you approach the wall. The wall interrupts your concentration and you have to start all over again to "groove" the movement. In a flume pool, once you establish the movement quality or sensation, you can just keep going for as many cycles as you like, a powerful aid to building the right kind of muscle memory.

- With no laps or repeats to count or pace clocks to focus on, in a flume pool, it's far easier to give all your attention to what *really* matters: how smooth and fluent your movements are and how you feel when your stroke is Fishlike. Thus, there's the potential of an almost Zen-like purity to the practice one can do in a moving current.

I plan to use my Endless Pool both for teaching and as a way of practicing my own swimming. I'm looking forward to being able to swim anytime I like, whether at 5 a.m. or 11 p.m., without leaving the house, and to enjoying the nirvana of one beautiful stroke after another for as long as I like.

Swim Tethers

A swim tether is a flexible line that you attach between yourself and the pool wall. Some are only long enough to allow you to move perhaps a few yards before halting your progress. Then you stroke in place at the end of your oversized rubber band for however long you want—perfect, some people feel, for training in a short backyard or hotel pool.

The idea sounds reasonable enough, letting you do your workout in a fraction of the space. But unfortunately, with a very short tether holding you in place the backward tension on your feet or ankles is so unnatural that it becomes almost impossible to do anything other than swim awkwardly, which is counterproductive for anyone working on skill. On the other hand, a swim tether that's long enough to let you swim all the way to the end of the pool (for a 25-yard pool this would be about 30 feet of relatively light tubing) can yield some useful lessons. Such a tether lets you swim against gradually increasing resistance—the last 5 yards can be very tough—as you move steadily forward.

The best thing you can do while wearing a swim tether is count your strokes, work on reducing your strokes per length (the total will obviously be higher than when swimming unimpeded), and play swimming golf. Use a sports watch to time yourself, add your stroke count to your time, and you have a score. On subsequent lengths, work on reducing it.

You can even practice sprinting. After you get all the way to the far end, rest at the wall (hang on tight!) for a moment, then turn around and swim back as fast as you can, the belt pulling you along faster than you could ever swim all by yourself. This is called *sprint-assisted* training, and it teaches your muscles to move faster than your best race pace.

But if you're working on your stroke count or your golf score, just float lazily back to the starting end, letting the cord do all the work. In just a minute, you'll need the energy you're saving to fight your way back down the pool again.

Two things you can say about swim training aids: You don't necessarily get what you pay for, and an idea that sounds good on paper or in ad copy doesn't necessarily make sense to your body. The simplest "pool tools" seem to work the best. And never forget that the simplest of all remains your own body.

PART THREE

Swimming for Life:

Be Healthy, Be Strong, Be Happy—Here's How

Swimming the Pounds Away

14

"Swimming? Absolutely the best all-around exercise. But if you want to lose weight, you need to run."

A lot of people still believe this, and a lot of people are wrong. It's an issue of more than passing interest to anyone who wants to shed a few pounds and prefers to spend most of his or her available exercise time in the pool. Actually, there's no scientific reason to be discouraged, and there's every reason to take heart.

Swimming has long suffered from a bad rep—especially compared to running and cycling—when it comes to weight control "Great exercise but no fat burner," repeat the skeptics, driving people unnecessarily onto the pavement in search of trimmer bodies. And you can understand how an unscientific sampling could seem to prove this. Just look at the number of gaunt runners slipping through the streets on a Saturday morning. Everyday athletes, not even elite champions.

But let's get scientific for a minute. The real question is, do swimming workouts burn as many calories—and as much fat—as running or biking? Several studies have suggested that they do not. But in each case the deck was stacked experimentally. The flaw common to all the studies was that the swimming, and the running to which it was compared, were not done at the same intensities. The swimming paces were far too slow to provide a reliable comparison.

Then, a 1989 study at the University of California at Davis finally compared the weight-loss effects of running and swimming on two groups, both of whom exercised at identical intensities: 75 percent of maximum capacity for every subject in both sports. And what do you suppose happened? The swimmers not only lost as much weight as the runners, they actually lost slightly more.

And four years later, Howard Wainer, a Princeton, New Jersey, swimmer who also happens to be a statistician calculated that champion swimmers burn about 25 percent *more* calories per hour than champion runners. Wainer's study, published in *Chance,* the journal of the American Statistical Association, suggested that swimming takes more energy because the drag forces of water are so much greater than air resistance on land, and also because swimmers work so many more muscles than runners.

Swimmers, of course, found none of this surprising. People who know the sport realize that elite swimmers are just as lean as elite athletes in any other sport. They simply look bigger than top runners, for example, because they *are* bigger. Fast swimming requires a powerful upper body, so swimmers' arm, chest, and back muscles are typically far more developed than those of runners or even cyclists.

So equal work produces equally lean bodies among serious athletes in swimming and other sports. But what about the obvious weight differences between casual swimmers and casual runners? In part, I'm convinced, it's a matter of simple psychology. Since your body weight in water is only 10 percent of what it is on land, an overweight runner feels every extra pound with every single step, while a chunky swimmer can be supremely comfortable. So, who has more motivation to watch what goes onto the plate?

Researchers have a more scientific explanation for the same eating behavior. Swimmers usually weigh more not because they burn fewer calories than other athletes, but because they *consume* more, says a study done by Dr. Grant Gwinup at the University of California at Irvine Medical Center. Gwinup's reasoning: Water at, say, 78 degrees Fahrenheit draws much more heat from the body than air at the same temperature. And swimmers' bodies react to that by adding protective insulation, which of course requires food to build up. My personal experience convinces me Dr. Gwinup is right. I never feel like eating after a run, while after swimming, I'm always primed to strap on the feedbag.

However, elite athlete or no, several strategies can help you both burn more fat while swimming *and* depress your post-swim-workout appetite when you're done. First, stay full-feeling simply by staying well hydrated (see "Hydration: When Swimmers Run Out of Water" on page 220). Drink ample fluids during the workout, which you should be doing anyway. Second, allow yourself some judicious snacking on filling but low-fat foods (such as fruit or fig bars) immediately after your swimming workout. That will tame your stoked-up appetite without piling on pounds.

How—and even when—you swim can affect the amount of fat you end up burning. During intense exercise, your muscles must rely on a very limited supply of stored energy. But swim with or using moderate effort and that all changes. Though it takes longer to burn the same number of calories at a slower pace, a greater percentage of the fuel being used is fat.

And physiologists now believe we can actually train our bodies to burn more fat even at higher intensities. The crossover point is usually

Swimming the Pounds Away

somewhere around 60 percent of an all-out effort—fairly low, actually—after which our burners switch over to carbohydrates as we work harder. But with the right training we can keep fat going into the furnace at efforts as high as 70 percent or even 80 percent of maximum.

Do this: Schedule a long swim practice (sixty to ninety minutes or even more) after eight to twelve hours of carbohydrate deprivation. The easiest way is to plan your workouts for the morning, before breakfast. By swimming easily for sixty to ninety minutes you'll burn more stored fat (Total Immersion intervals can do this as well as nonstop swimming can—they just have to be *easy* intervals), and the more you repeat this routine, the more you'll condition your body to use fat rather than stored muscle energy (called glycogen) as fuel.

Need more of a carrot to do that much work on an empty stomach? Here it is: That University of California at Davis study also showed that prolonged, easy aerobic training sessions give you an impressive afterburn, boosting your metabolism so you continue burning extra calories for up to twelve hours after you finish your workout.

Bottom line: You *can* lose weight in the pool. Any swimmer having trouble with the pounds ought to blame his fork, not his sport.

Hydration: When Swimmers Run Out of Water

Earlier in this book, I promised you could become a very good swimmer with nothing more than your suit, cap, and goggles. No added equipment necessary.

Not quite. One piece of equipment should always be sitting on the deck at the end of your lane: your water bottle. It's easy, and common, to mistakenly figure that because your sweat isn't obvious, it's not happening. But you not only sweat during a swim workout, you sweat copiously.

Prove it by weighing yourself before and after a workout. You've lost weight, of course, and it's all water. Sweat losses of as little as 2 percent of your body weight (just 3 pounds for a 150-pound swimmer) can cut dramatically into your performance. In fact, dehydration is far more likely to slow you down than running out of muscle energy, making "water loading" even more important than carbo loading.

But plain water is not always the liquid of choice. A study by Dr. Jack Wilmore, an exercise physiologist at the University of Texas, found that for workouts of less than an hour, nothing beats water. If you're going longer, fluid replacement sports drinks that contain electrolytes (salts) are absorbed into your bloodstream faster than water, which means better performance and a faster recovery when you're done.

Their formulas are all slightly different, so I can only repeat the standard coach's advice: experiment. Some may agree with you and others may not. I found one that tastes good to me and sits well in my stomach, and I've noticed a marked boost during the second half of any seventy-five-minute workout since I've started using it.

The Smart Swimmer's Drinking Rules

1. You can sweat off 6 to 8 ounces of fluid every fifteen minutes—yes, even in the pool. That's a healthy swig from your water bottle every quarter hour.

2. Want to be more precise? Weigh yourself before and after a workout. Each pound lost is a pint (16 ounces) of water gone out of you. Next time, bring that much in your water bottle(s).

3. Prehydrate. Drink 2 to 3 cups of water (16 to 24 ounces) about two hours before swimming and another 2 cups fifteen minutes before your workout.

4. Drink *before* you're thirsty. Thirst means your body already needs water, so it's too late to prevent dehydration. This is especially true for older swimmers, since after middle age we feel less thirsty as we dry out and the body's warning signals can be overlooked.

Shedding Pounds in the Pool: How to Swim to Burn the Most Fat

Is swimming an effective exercise for losing weight? It certainly is, despite all the theories to the contrary that have come and gone. We now know this: If you burn more calories than you eat, you will drop pounds—on an exercise bike, at the track, or in the pool. And swimming is one of the most comfortable ways to burn calories you'll ever find.

So if slimming down by reducing body fat, improving your cholesterol count, and helping lower blood pressure are important goals for your exercise program, you've come to the right sport. And believe it or not, the best way to do all of that, plus improve your stroke technique, is with easy swimming, the keystone of Total Immersion swimming.

Research has proven that exercising moderately (at just 60 percent of your maximum heart rate) provides the same health benefits as hard workouts as long as you cover the same distance. That's health, mind you, in contrast to performance. Obviously, if you want to win a championship by swimming faster than everyone else, you'll still have to do intense work. But it's not an essential ingredient to keeping your cardiovascular system tuned up.

In a six-month study at the Cooper Institute for Aerobics Research in Dallas, a group of women who walked three miles daily at a slow pace gained the same health benefits as a group that walked the same distance much faster. In fact, walking burns just as many calories per mile as running. It just takes longer to cover the same distance.

Michael Pollock, Ph.D., director of the Human Performance Laboratory at the University of Florida, found that slow walking was also just as effective as fast walking at reducing body fat, high blood pressure, and cholesterol. And at the Cooper Institute, the strollers actually lost more body fat than the power walkers.

None of this is surprising, since researchers have long known the best way to burn fat is to exercise at lower intensities for longer periods of time. Our bodies use two main fuels to supply energy: fats (which we'd like to burn more of) and carbohydrates (which our bodies, left to their own devices, would like to burn more of; carbohydrates are more efficient, after all). Long, easy practices are one way to get the body to draw a greater percentage of the energy it needs from fats than it would if you sped things up.

CONTINUED

Swimming the Pounds Away

"The total amount of work you do ends up being the important factor," says Pollock. "People can go slower. They just need to go longer to get the same results."

Well, that's certainly easy enough. If you swim a mile at an average pace of 1:30 per 100 yards, you'll finish the practice in only 27 minutes. At 2:00 per 100 yards, you'll be done in 36 minutes. But you obviously can't cut back both pace *and* distance. Less is less. Even the American College of Sports Medicine, which now advises that it's okay to work at less than 60 percent of maximal capacity, stipulates that you must still do it long enough and frequently enough to get the benefit. For adult swimmers, this would mean about 6000 to 8000 yards of swimming a week, in three to four pool sessions.

So there's nothing wrong with discovering that easing your pace a little makes it easier to get to the pool in the first place. Higher-intensity exercise programs inevitably suffer from higher dropout rates because people just don't enjoy them and get frustrated when they can't "measure up." "By encouraging slower, more comfortable exercise," says Dr. Pollock, "we're giving people a reason *to* exercise rather than an excuse not to."

No argument from me. After all, easy swimming is also the perfect pace for Total Immersion practice. You can do your drills and technique work and count your strokes per length much more effectively at low intensity than when you're trying to burn up the pool.

Even interval training, normally done with a little more gusto, can become a "fat burner." Just use a more relaxed pace. You won't need much rest between repeats because your heart rate will stay fairly even at moderate paces, but even brief rests are beneficial—especially for adult swimmers—since they control the levels of fatigue-producing lactic acid that accumulates in muscles and the bloodstream. That in turn means less stiffness and soreness after your workout. And interval repeats with their built-in rest periods help the heart supply more blood, oxygen, and nutrients to joints and muscles, reducing your chance of hurting something.

But how fast is "slow enough"? To calculate your easygoing, pound-dropping, health-building clip for intervals, multiply your best 100-yard time by anywhere from 1.25 to 1.5. So if your best time is 1:20, you'll be right on target at a pace between 1:40 and 2:00 per 100. Plan on ten to twenty seconds of rest between swims. And if you're doing stroke drills rather than straight swimming, your times will naturally fall in the upper part of the range. Use the same formula to figure your pace for repeats of other distances. Or just follow the Total Immersion practices in the appendix. Done as suggested, they work well as both stroke builders and fat burners.

To enjoy the optimum fat-burning benefit, just add enough repeats or sets to allow for at least an hour in the pool. But as you do so, keep in mind the potential conflict between longer sessions (to burn more fat) and quality skill work (to become a better swimmer). If you can't maintain good form for an hour or more, you may have to choose one priority over another. If it's becoming a better swimmer, don't stretch the practice to the point where fatigue hurts your form, just so you can burn a few more calories. Instead add thirty minutes of walking or biking or treadmill or exercise bike or anything that simply burns calories and fat but doesn't depend on maintaining good form.

Staying Strong, Supple, and Injury-Free: "Dryland Training" the Total Immersion Way

My goal with this book has been to guide you on what to do in the pool, so I won't attempt to provide the last word on what coaches call "dryland training." But Total Immersion, as much as a way of swimming, also means a philosophy of intelligent and practical exercise. Plus, if you have come to this book as a relatively new swimmer, you deserve at least a "quick-start guide" of the sort that comes with a new computer. So I will suggest a range of exercise options with three goals:

- Dryland supplements to the gravity-free exercise of water, essential to a strong musculoskeletal system

- "Prehab" exercises to keep your shoulders—a swimmer's most vulnerable joint—healthy and pain-free

- Basic guidance on sensible strength training that will help your body perform optimally while doing swimming movements.

And while I'll just present the basics here, I'll suggest resources for deeper study in the appendix.

Preventing Shoulder Injury: A Quick and Simple Plan

Swimming deserves its reputation for being both vigorous and gentle. But "gentle" doesn't guarantee "injury-free," particularly when it comes to your shoulder, which is almost ideally built for trouble. Shoulder anatomy looks like a racquetball (the head of your upper arm bone) balanced on a bottle cap (the socket of the scapula). The ball is held on the bottle cap by a network of seventeen muscles. This is great for mobility, but terrible for accelerating your arm rearward against resistance. "Swimmer's shoulder" is common among swimmers because "human swimmers" instinctively try to muscle the water— rather than anchor the hand and let their core body do most of the work. The resulting overstretched rotator cuff muscles allow the arm bone (a.k.a. the humerus) to wobble in its socket. This pinches the muscles and tendons that stabilize your shoulder, causing inflammation and pain.

Because a swimmer's shoulder rotates 1,200 to 1,500 times every mile, a prevention plan is clearly in order. The most important muscles to strengthen are the rotator cuff muscles, which stabilize the head of the humerus, allowing the other shoulder muscles to perform effectively, and the scapular (shoulder blade) stabilizers, which protect against pinched tendons and rotator cuff stress. The primary virtue of this routine is that it requires little time (ten minutes, three times per week) and little equipment. All you need for those exercises specifying the use of resistance is stretch cords, a Thera-Band, or light weights—keep resistance light enough to do at least 10 to 15 repetitions of each exercise. Work until you feel fatigue; rest and do a second set, for a total of at least 20 to 30 reps of each. Over t[

build to 30 or more repetitions in a single set (no second se

when you do) before fatigue.

STRENGTHEN YOUR ROTATOR CUFF MUSCLES

EXERCISE 1. Stand with arms at your sides, a dumbbell in each hand. Roll your shoulders forward, up toward your ears, back, then down again, moving through the greatest possible range of movement. Alternate one front-to-back rotation with one in the opposite direction.

EXERCISE 2. Lie on your side with your head propped on your hand and your top arm against your side, bent at a right angle with knuckles forward and palm down, holding a light weight. Keep the upper arm against your body as you slowly rotate your forearm until your knuckles point to the sky then return at the same speed. You can also do this exercise while standing, with stretch cords or a Thera-Band for resistance. Hold your arms close to your body in a "shake-hands" position with your elbows held into your ribs. (Place a thin cushion or pillow between elbow and ribs for greater stability.) Grasp the ends of the cords or Thera-Band in your hands. Rotate your forearms slowly out to the side, then return at the same speed.

EXERCISE 3. Sit or stand with your arms straight and hanging at your side. Leading with your thumb, slowly raise your arms to just below and just in front of your shoulder, pause for a moment, then return at the same speed. Use a light weight of 5 to 8 pounds, a Thera-Band, or cords for resistance.

EXERCISE 4. Bend at the waist, with your arms hanging straight

Staying Strong, Supple, and Injury-Free

from your shoulders. (Soften your knees to avoid lower-back strain.) Leading with your knuckles and slightly-bent elbows, raise your arms slowly to shoulder level, pause for a moment, then return at the same speed.

STRENGTHEN YOUR SCAPULAR STABILIZERS

EXERCISE 1. Sit on a chair with armrests and with your feet flat on the floor. Place your hands on the armrests. Straighten your elbows and push down, lifting your hips off the chair. (If necessary, help by pushing a bit with your feet; as you get stronger let your arms do more of the work.) You can do this one at work!

EXERCISE 2. Place your hands on a stable surface (counter, desk, the back of a couch, almost anything that's three to four feet high). Position your feet so that you are in a semistanding "push-up" position with your head and spine aligned, hands at shoulder width, and arms straight. Do a slow push-up—*but without bending your elbows.* Keep your arms straight, and lower your chest a few inches as your shoulder blades pinch together. Then, using shoulder muscles, press back up, rounding your shoulders and spreading your shoulder blades as much as possible. As you grow stronger, move toward a more horizontal position, eventually doing it in a push-up or "plank" position.

EXERCISE 3. Attach a Thera-Band or cords to a stable object at waist or chest height. Grasp the ends and with your arms straight in front and your shoulders down away from your ears, pull your shoulders back (pinching shoulder blades together), then return them forward at the same speed, until you feel your shoulder blades stretch wide. Move slowly enough to feel the muscles in the middle of your back contract and relax.

EXERCISE 4. Lie on your stomach, with a rolled towel under your forehead and a pillow under your hips. Extend your arms forward from your shoulders (biceps two inches from your ears), elbows straight and thumbs up. Raise your arms as far as possible, without bending your elbows; hold them at their highest point for a moment, then lower slowly. Feel the effort from your shoulders to the middle of your back. Start with no weight; work up to 2 to 5 pounds.

EXERCISE 5. Lie on your stomach, with a rolled towel under your forehead and a pillow under your hips. Extend your arms to the sides at shoulder level with palms down or forward, (thumbs pointing up). Keeping elbows straight, pinch your shoulder blades together as you lift your arms; pause at the highest point for a moment, then lower slowly. Do this with or without light weights.

STRETCH THE MUSCLES UNDER THE SHOULDER

Swimming promotes natural flexibility and fights the stiffness of aging better than any other sport, but it's not enough by itself. In fact, even in "body-friendly" TI swimming, your shoulder muscles still do an important job holding your hand/arm in a leveraged position so you can move past that spot. They'll benefit from being stretched after contracting repetitively for an hour or so. The six stretches described here, which target the muscles you use most, will keep you feeling loose and supple. Do one or both of each pair of exercises while in the shower after swimming, holding each for about ten yoga breaths.

STRETCH 1. Raise one arm above your head, dropping your hand behind your shoulder. Lean the back of your elbow against a corner of a wall and press until you feel a stretch from the elbow down to your armpit and below.

STRETCH 2. Put both arms overhead in the streamlined position. Lean first to the left side as far as possible, then to the right. Feel the pull all the way down your side.

STRETCH THE MUSCLES IN FRONT OF THE SHOULDER

STRETCH 1. Hold one arm out to your side at a right angle; bend your elbow 90 degrees with fingers up and palm forward. Brace the inside surface of your hand, forearm, and elbow against a doorway with your elbow at shoulder height. As you press your arm against the doorway, turning your opposite hip back until you feel a stretch across the front of your shoulder and upper chest. Repeat with your elbow braced at ear level.

STRETCH 2. Put both arms behind your back. Grasp your hands together with fingers interlaced, fists resting against your buttocks and shoulder blades pinched. Slowly raise your arms upward behind you as far as possible. When you can't raise them any further, bend forward from the waist and continue, trying to raise them toward vertical.

STRETCH THE MUSCLES IN BACK OF THE SHOULDER

STRETCH 1. Place the back of your hand on your lower back (the palm of your hand facing back) with your elbow out to the side. Your fingertips point toward the opposite hip. Brace the inside of your elbow against a doorway, while turning your opposite hip forward. Allow your elbow to move forward until you feel a stretch across the back of your shoulder.

STRETCH 2. Put your right arm across your body so that the shoulder is under your chin and your right hand, forearm, and upper arm parallel to the ground. Wrap your left arm outside the right, so your left wrist is behind your right elbow. Pull in steadily with the left arm, pressing the right as close to your chest as possible. Then switch.

Functional Strength Training

Many swimmers are tempted to think they can overpower the water by bulking up. But water, being a fluid medium, just doesn't respond to sheer power. The water's resistance will always surpass any strength you can apply and, besides, it takes a special kind of strength, accurately applied, to overcome the water's resistance.

The world's best swimmers don't have bulky or highly defined muscles. The strength that produces world records, as well as helping anyone to swim efficiently, fluently, and enjoyably is more like that exhibited by the slim, graceful cables that hold up the Brooklyn Bridge than by the brutes who heft enormous poundage in weight-lifting competitions. Which is not to say that conventional weight lifting has no value for swimmers. Anyone beyond their middle thirties should do some form of resistance training twice a week, purely for health, according to the American College of Sports Medicine. If you do go to a gym, rather than focus on "swimming-specific muscles," ask a trainer to help plan a program of compound/complex exercises for general strength development.

What is probably of greatest value to your swimming is "functional strength," the kind that makes us more robust in everything from spading the garden to shoveling the walk to swimming 1500 meters. And that means training muscles and joints to work as they do when we move—multiple muscle groups, multiple joints, and complex planes of movement, all at once. This is because fast swimming isn't produced by muscling your way through the water, but by maintaining body positions that minimize drag and connect the propelling armstrokes to the power of the core body's "kinetic chain." That kind of strength is developed by practicing challenging movements that teach torso and arm/shoulder muscles to work together. Since my mid-forties, I've begun the regular practice of yoga, which I've found to be a more integrated form of exercise than a myriad of other activities each focused on something different, like, say weight lifting, sit-ups, and stretching.

My yoga practice feels utterly functional for swimming because it teaches me to use my body as a system, working all muscle groups in unison, against the resistance of gravity and my own inflexibility to build strength and flexibility with each movement. Exercises such as push-ups, pull-ups, dips, step-ups, and squats, done with just the weight of your own body, also develop muscle sense and joint stability, letting tendons and ligaments adapt rather than being overwhelmed as they sometimes are by machines or external weight.

Especially critical to functional strength is "core strength," which means strength in the abdominal muscles, spinal rotators and erectors, hip flexors, the glutes, and more. If your core isn't strong, then neither are you, because your torso is the force coupler that transmits power from legs to upper body. Abdominal exercises of all sorts, and particularly Pilates exercises develop core power. I take Pilates classes with a certified instructor and practice on my own with the aid of a book. (See resources for more information on yoga and Pilates.)

On the Ball

One of the best developers of functional and core strength is stability ball exercise. And not incidentally, stability ball exercises are among the most enjoyable ways to get a workout because they lend almost any exercise routine a childlike sense of play. But that's not to say they don't offer serious benefits, because they do.

The primary benefit of these large, inflatable vinyl balls is that they add a critical dimension to anything you do on them: *in*stability. Because the ball tends to wobble or roll as you exercise on it, your body recruits bands of muscle radiating out from your core toward your extremities to keep you balanced and stable. Some examples:

- When I do push-ups with the ball under my knees, in addition to the chest and back muscles that typically do the work in a push-up, I can also feel muscles from my shoulders to my hips working to keep me from rolling off to the side.

- When I do a "bench press" with dumbbells, resting my upper back and shoulders on the ball. I can feel my abdominals supporting my torso as well as my thighs and hip flexors stabilizing me.

- When I do a body-weight squat, with the ball between my back and a wall, my hip muscles are working to keep me aligned.

- And when I do abdominal curls, with the ball supporting my lower back, I'm aware of my front and side abdominals stabilizing my midsection to a far greater degree than when I do sit-ups on an exercise mat.

Recent research at the biomechanics lab at San Diego State University confirms what my own muscles tell me. Stability balls were found to be particularly effective at working torso muscles in functional combinations. There's that word *functional* again. Virtually every stability ball exercise I've done (and they are versatile enough to integrate with almost any kind of exercise) has given me the same sense of muscle function that I feel when swimming—body extended in a horizontal position with muscles from fingertips to toes working dynamically to counteract the forces of gravity and drag. The stability ball may be the best dryland simulator yet for that kind of challenge. And you'll never find it boring.

Here's one of my favorite series.

To Begin. Balance in a horizontal position with the ball below your hips, hands directly under your shoulders, and legs straight behind, parallel to the floor.

ACTION. Walk your hands out until the ball is at your knees. Pause for two slow breaths, then walk back. Repeat 5 to 10 times.

KEY POINT. Maintain a straight, horizontal line from your shoulders to your feet.

"ADVANCED PLACEMENT": Try any of the following:

1. Walk out until the ball is under your knees, then pause and do a push-up. Lower your chest down toward the floor—your legs and feet will rise; keep the line from shoulders to feet straight. Press back up to horizontal, then walk it back to your hips.

2. Walk out until the ball is under your shins or ankles, then walk it back to your hips. Don't let your back sway or bend; keep your hips in line with your spine and feet.

3. With the ball under your knees, roll it under your left knee, then under your right. You'll feel muscles in the side of your shoulder and upper back working to keep you on the ball.

In each of these exercises you'll be aware of contracting a connected band of muscle from your hands to your hips—exactly the way you should feel your strength while swimming. The variations will each recruit different stabilizer muscles into the action. This training is as swimming-functional as anything you can do on land.

Your Friends Are Waiting ("Who Can I Swim With? And Where?")

16

Though long-distance running is supposedly the sport of loneliness—at least the short-story title tells us so—a good case could also be made for swimming. Think about it. You can't hear much but your own breathing, conversation is out of the question, and the view is pretty much limited to the pool walls and bottom. Hard to imagine a more solitary way to exercise.

Or a more friendly one, either. Perhaps it's a reaction to that private little cocoon we do all our laps in, but swimmers as a group are wonderfully congenial. And that's a good thing, because it's often easier to become truly proficient as a member of a group than alone. Thanks to the extensive network of local, regional, and national groups, nearly anyone can join.

Even if you're not a "joiner," you may want to rethink a purely solo practice schedule. I swim alone most of the time too, but when I can practice with friends, I swim faster and enjoy the camaraderie. Faster because even friendly competition gives you a push—it's just good, healthy instinct to race a little when someone's in the lane next to yours. Enjoyable because no matter how blissful my solo practices are, I also enjoy the company of like-minded swimmers. And though joining Masters swimming is a good way of finding them, you can assure the maximum compatibility and congeniality by simply gathering a group of friends. As your Total Immersion skills grow, you're going to enjoy swimming more and more—probably for a long time to come. You'll grow faster, and enjoy the journey more, with the company of those who like to practice in a similarly purposeful and mindful way.

Swimming With Friends/Finding Friends to Swim With

THE BUDDY SYSTEM

Find a compatible training partner (or two or three) and make a pact to meet at the pool one or more times a week. Not only will you feel more obliged to keep the appointment and end up swimming more regularly, you'll both swim better with company.

You'll probably soon find you weren't alone looking for training mates, as your little band grows. One winter I decided I needed the push of meeting a couple of friends to work out at 6:30 each morning. Frequently, our "workout circle" grew by five or six people as other stray predawn exercisers asked if they too could "join up." Casual team formation like this is the most convenient and flexible way to gain the benefits of swimming with other people. You can even get some impromptu coaching, since workout mates are always happy to watch you stroke or drill. Just tell them what you're practicing and what to look for, preferably underwater through goggles.

JOINING MASTERS SWIMMING

Don't be put off by the word *Masters.* It doesn't mean what you may think, as I'll explain in a moment.

Joining a Masters team, in fact, is probably the best way to swim with friends of all abilities and make new ones. You'll also have a coach to plan your workouts and help you improve your stroke, though there's a wide range of professionalism, energy, and attention levels among Masters coaches. Some seem to have a gift for making every practice better than the one before. Others are little more than lifeguards. You won't know until you try, though asking members before you join usually produces reliable opinions. You do lose some flexibility in scheduling your swim with a Masters group, but you can always practice with the team when it's convenient, and on your own when it's not.

Above all, know that "Masters" is not a code word for "serious" or "elite." A tiny percentage of Masters swimmers fit that description, but most probably swim just like you do—or they did until they joined a Masters team and jump-started their progress. In fact, only a third of Masters swimmers compete. Most join with no intention of ever racing. They're strictly fitness and recreational swimmers who love the sport, want to meet other people who do too, and are looking for coaching to help them along.

It's a personal and personable organization. For though U.S. Masters Swimming is the national administrative body, the grassroots foundation—all most swimmers ever see anyway—are the fifty Local Masters Swim Committees (LMSC) that oversee Masters swimming groups in their areas. The LMSCs handle registration, organize and sanction meets, maintain regular communications with their members,

Your Friends Are Waiting

and often have social activities as well. The national office coordinates among the LMSCs, organizes National and Postal meets (see box), and provides insurance for all members. For more information on U.S. Masters Swimming, visit www.usms.org where you'll find a link for for your area's LMSC and a directory of places to swim all over the country.

Masters groups run the gamut from loose and informal to highly structured. Most groups include swimmers of both kinds and many in between, all swimming happily under the same roof. In one or two lanes, you'll find former competitive swimmers who train intensely, whether for meets or for fitness. In the intermediate lanes, swimmers who came to the sport a little later, and who suit up for the occasional Masters meet (plus triathletes who are usually quite competitive but less experienced as swimmers). And in the rest, fitness swimmers who joined mainly for coaching pointers and camaraderie. If your skills are sound (i.e., you can consistently swim an average of twenty strokes per length), you will almost certainly find a lane that suits you.

Larger teams usually offer more practices and more coaches. Smaller groups may offer fewer practices and less experienced coaches, but more opportunity for one-on-one advice. And one thing most have in common—a life outside the pool. Masters teams tend to be quite social. In the end, you'll probably choose the group that offers the most convenient practice location and schedule.

RULES OF THE ROAD IN THE POOL

Pools are not like parks. You can't just throw a bunch of athletes in and let them work out any way they please. Space is too tight, lanes are too confining. So swimmers observe an unspoken but certainly not unofficial etiquette that is not only polite but practical, fitting in as many people as possible, doing the workouts they need safely, smoothly, and without collisions.

The sooner you know the rules, the better you'll fit in wherever you find yourself swimming. Fortunately, just like the rules of the road for cars, the conventions in pools are pretty similar all over the United States, which means you should be able to fit in smoothly anywhere. But just to be sure, check with the lifeguard at any unfamiliar pool. They may have invented something new there.

1. Picking your lane. In a busy pool, specific lanes are usually reserved for faster, moderate, and slower-speed swimmers, and are often identified by signs on the wall, deck, or starting block. Of course, those speed terms are relative. "Fast" could mean 1:00 per 100 yards in one pool, 1:30 in another. So your best bet is to eyeball each lane and pick the one that looks most like you. Worry about labels some other time.

If no directions are posted, then it's kind of frontier justice: Possession is nine tenths of the law. Whoever's already there sets the lane's pace. If you're faster than the pacesetters, back off. Today might be a good time to work on your stroke instead of your speed.

CONTINUED

Your Friends Are Waiting

You'll certainly be swimming more slowly during the first five or ten minutes as you warm up, so you may want to start in a slower lane, then switch to a faster one later. Or, if you've been swimming for a while and decide to do a kicking set which will slow you down, it makes sense to switch lanes.

2. Getting in. Rule one: No diving. Ever. It's not safe, and even if you happen to think it is, the pool's insurance company disagrees. Lower yourself down gently, feet first, anywhere lap swimming is going on.

Then, don't just barge in. You'll be sharing tight space with strangers, and pushing off whenever you feel like it is no way to show goodwill and cooperation. If someone is obviously in the middle of a long swim and won't be stopping anytime soon, slip into the pool and stand to the side of the lane for a minute or so, allowing them see you before you start. And never push off immediately in front of or behind someone else. Allow at least five or ten seconds of cushion either way.

3. Navigating. If there's just one other swimmer in the lane, you two can split it if you want, each taking a side. It's first-come, first-served, so ask as you're getting in whether your lane mate would prefer to "circle" or "split." With three or more, there's obviously no choice but to circle. So if you'll be the third and the first two are splitting, slip in, stand to one side until they both notice you, and ask if they'd mind switching to a circle pattern.

Circling is nearly always counterclockwise—at least in countries where we drive on the right. In left-driving countries, I've found they swim the same way: clockwise. Think of the line on the bottom as the highway divider and stay to the right, as close to the lane rope as possible.

CONTINUED

Swimming for Life

4. Passing. Sometimes, even with everyone in a lane supposedly moving along at the same clip, you'll come steaming up on someone's soles. To pass, tap him on the feet *only once* during the lap. When you reach the next wall, he'll move right and you'll pass on the left. If you are the "passee," of course, yield by moving to the right at the next wall.

Don't be stubborn when you're doing intervals. It's everyone's pool, and to make that work you may have to be flexible enough to adjust your timing up or down to give other swimmers some space. Slower swimmer coming in toward the end of your interval countdown? Shave your rest a little and leave before they get there, instead of pushing off the instant they go by and immediately having to pass. If a faster swimmer's coming in, extend your interval a few seconds so you push off behind them, rather than getting in their way.

Common sense and awareness will get you everywhere. If a swimmer behind you is coming up fast enough to catch you on the next length, don't even wait until she taps your feet. Stop at the next wall and let her by. Good manners are always appreciated. And almost always reciprocated.

5. Resting. To take a breather, squeeze into the right-side corner (your right as you swim toward the wall). To take a long breather, more than a couple of minutes, sit on the deck completely out of the way.

So much for the actual swimming part. On the deck: (1) Never loiter in front of the pace clock. After all, people can't read through you. And (2) Don't borrow the equipment sitting at the end of the lane without asking, even if it looks like it's not being used.

Masters Swim Meets: You Can't Lose

These days I'm actually surprised when a new swimmer even mentions wanting to enter a Masters meet or open-water race someday. New runners seem ready to fill out their first road race application the minute their Nikes are broken in. What is it about swim meets that makes lap swimmers—even those who have been at it for decades—think the contests are just for experts? If runners were such pessimists, every 10K race would be over in a blink, maybe under forty minutes. No one who took longer would bother showing up.

Swimmers don't know what they're missing. After you've been practicing your Total Immersion drills for a while, and your stroke has begun to feel smoother, easier, and faster, the best way to test your progress is swimming in a Masters meet.

"But I'm not in it for the medals," you say. Good. Neither are most other Masters. The best way to once and for all explode the myth that Masters meets are for bloodthirsty award hounds is to watch one. Grassroots pastime or National Championship, you'll see competitors of all ages who might not stand out in any YMCA lap session. True, the whiz kids might knock off 100 yards of freestyle in under fifty seconds, but others may take three minutes . . . and they'll get hearty applause for a job well done.

What most astonishes former college swimmers like me, people who remember meets as pressure-cooker contests of grim determination, is the relaxed, folksy feeling at Masters meets. Having a good time comes first, turning in a good time comes second. Competition is against the clock, not against each other.

Most people don't talk about why they won't race. People who admit their reluctance to enter Masters meets often describe feeling intimidated by the thought of facing these expectations:

1. *You must execute a racing start off a high platform.* No you mustn't. Masters swimmers are free to start their races in the water—and often do, simply because they feel more comfortable that way.

2. *You have to be able to do racing flip turns.* Wrong again. The easily learned open turn is common at Masters meets. I've seen swimmers in older age groups win national titles with them.

3. *You'll be racing against former collegiate stars.* Nonsense. First, only a third of the swimmers at Masters meets have had any pre-Masters competitive swimming experience. Second, if you're new to this, you'll be swimming with other new swimmers anyway since heats are seeded by estimated time. Many meets even offer novice-only races, restricted to those who have never swum the event competitively. You could be a medalist your first time out.

It generally works this way: At meets, men and women are divided into five-year age groups for scoring purposes, beginning with nineteen to twenty-four and continuing up to one hundred plus. But heats are normally seeded according to time, with no regard for age or sex. A twenty-four-year-old woman could be swimming next to a sixty-two-year-old man if their times are expected to be similar.

In fact, you're ready for a Masters meet if you can swim two lengths of a 25-yard pool in good form (50 yards is the minimum distance in Masters meets). Most people can finish off a 50-yard race in 30 seconds to a minute. Freestyle and backstroke are the least technical events. Forget breaststroke and butterfly for now. Legal breaststroke requires a frog-like kick that feels ungainly to many novices and as for butterfly, even two lengths is a challenge for anyone.

And when Masters say freestyle, they mean *freestyle*. As in free to choose any style you like. Most of us use the so-called crawl because it's generally fastest, but you're the boss. In 1992, I watched two ninety-something gentlemen race neck-and-neck in a 200-meter freestyle contest in the Masters World Championships. Both were using an elementary backstroke, perfectly legal under the rules.

Finally, pick any event distance you want—right up to the longest, which is the 1500-meter freestyle, just this side of a mile—so long as you can complete the race without standing up or holding on to lane lines. Masters National and even World Championships are all-comers meets, with competitors usually guaranteed the right to swim in three events without meeting any qualifying times. Local, state, and even regional meets never require qualifying times for entry to any number of events.

Don't mistakenly think the best ways to ease into swim racing are the short 50- or 100-yard events because they're over fast. Shorter races take more skill, power, and speed to avoid being left way behind. You're better off going maybe 500 yards, which also gives you time to work on things you've been practicing, like form and pace. Besides, it will feel more like your practice swimming than the breakneck speed of a short sprint.

You needn't be in superb shape to handle 500 yards, either. Remember our "Rule of 70": 70 percent of your swim performance comes from your stroke mechanics and only 30 percent from fitness. Once you can swim for about eight minutes nonstop in a practice, you probably have a 500-yard event inside.

MAIL-IN MEETS: THE FIRST-CLASS STAMP SWIMMING TEST

Want a race all your own? No spectators, no specific starting time, no noise, no pressure? Postal meets (you just mail in your results and officials handle the scoring) are as no-pressure as they get. Betty Barry of Victor, New York, directed a postal meet called the Fitness Challenge for several years and says a third of her entrants are people who have never been in any kind of organized swimming event before. "One woman sent me a note with her entry that said, 'I don't want to get up on the blocks; I don't want to have to race anybody; I'm so happy that you've given me the opportunity to do something meaningful by myself in my own pool.' "

Like a chess match played by mail, you never meet your rivals face to face in a postal event. Swim in whatever pool suits you, at your own convenience, the only required spectator being a lap counter/timer of your choice. When you're done, write your result on the entry form, have your witness sign it, and mail it to the tabulator. A couple of weeks later, you're notified how you placed against everyone else who did the same thing. It's as private and civilized as an unpublished phone number.

And more varied than a "real" meet. Short events, long events, one for the maximum distance swum in one hour, another for the grand total of your February yardage. Awards are always tabulated by gender and five-year age group, as they are in regular Masters meets.

Postal events can juice up your training with the motivation that can come only from entering a race. And they're real money savers. You can compare yourself to other swimmers your age from all over the country without ever having to buy a plane ticket. Check the USMS Web site (www.usms.org) for a schedule of postal events.

No Lanes, No Walls—The Wide-Open-Water Swim

Open-water swims are not all as "clubby" as Masters meets, but they're just as relaxing in their own way. And it's for the same reason that road races are so much more popular than track meets among runners— freedom of the "open road" and the happy anonymity of competing in a field of hundreds.

Just as thousands of foot-powered athletes would never consider the military regimentation of a track meet, open-water competitions draw swimmers who never race in a pool. Without the intimidation of timers standing watchfully around the deck, rivals challenging from neighboring starting blocks, and bleachers full of curious fans peering at the water—maybe even at you—open-water events are as matter-of-fact as a weekend 10K. Proof: Though U.S. Masters Swimming has some 40,000 registered members, only a third enter meets as we said earlier. Yet 60,000 people swim in open-water races connected with triathlons each year, and thousands more crowd the shorelines at open-water swims. Who needs the coddled precision of lanes? For the price of an occasional foot in the face or elbow in the ear from one of the other unguided bodies, you have freedom.

So why is it many swimmers never venture out of the pool to explore the exhilaration of swimming in lakes, rivers, and oceans? Timidity. Swimming without a line to guide you, a bottom you can see, and a wall nearby for comfort? Buoys you have to find so you don't get lost, perhaps surf to fight, and who knows what else in the water out there besides swimmers? No thanks.

All manageable risks, and clearly worth the managing when you finally plunge in off the beach and your body remembers that before chlorine, before filters and pumps, even before electric lights, this is how we swam. There may be no wall to touch for security, but there's no wall hemming you in either.

Obviously without the customary safety net of lifeguards, bottoms to stand on, and walls or lane markers to hold on to, you've got to ready a safety net of your own. Here's how to put it in place.

Feeling at Home at Sea: Strategies

BACK AT THE POOL

You'll adapt to open-water conditions much faster if you first sharpen a couple of skills in the pool.

1. Practice bilateral breathing. You can't be certain of getting air on your more comfortable side during an open-water race. Wind and waves may be against you, and your landmarks may be on your "other" side, so you need to be able to roll your head either way at any time.

2. Practice swimming and looking up and forward two to three times per pool length. Visualize what you're looking for *before* you lift your head. This will teach you to spot your landmarks right away, holding on to your rhythm and balance as you do.

3. Swim some 25-yard repeats with your eyes closed to test your ability to swim straight when the water's murky and there's nothing to guide on. Do this slowly in case you run into a lane line, and wait until you have a lane to yourself unless you enjoy getting a reputation as an unguided torpedo. Count strokes and open your eyes when you calculate you're still four short of the wall. No accidents please. This will teach you to swim straight without a lane line for guidance.

BEFORE THE RACE

1. Obviously you want to do some swimming in a lake or the ocean first. You'll get used to the absence of convenient guides like lane lines, and will learn to navigate instinctively using on-shore landmarks. *Safety first:* Swim with an experienced partner or in a group, or with an escort canoe or kayak. Be careful in cold water and stay close to shore. Hypothermia (lowered body temperature) can impair your coordination and cloud your judgment. A wetsuit, if you have one, will be good insulation.

ON RACE DAY

1. If you can't swim out and check the course itself, at least study a map. Picture how important landmarks—notably the finish line—will look from the water. Check with the lifeguards for water temperature, prevailing currents, and, if it's an ocean race, surf conditions.

2. Count how many buoys you have to pass or turn on, and on which side you need to pass them. Check bottom contours for the areas where you'll be entering and leaving the water. How far can you run and "porpoise," and where will you need to start swimming?

3. If wetsuits are allowed in the race, wear one. You'll swim about 5 percent faster without working any harder for it.

DURING THE RACE

1. Open-water races usually begin with a mass (confusion) start. Stay off to the side, even if you have to swim a slightly longer course to the first buoy. You'll be out of the middle of the pack, where a collision with a stray arm or leg could ruin your rhythm, knock your goggles off, or in rare cases, do some damage.

2. Look for someone slightly faster than you are to draft off. Drafting will let you swim a little faster with no more exertion, not to mention letting you get away with lifting your head for navigation much less often. You can just keep your face in the water and follow the pack. You can, that is, if your draftee knows where he's going.

3. You may need to adjust your stroke for ocean swimming. Don't worry. Methodical pool swimmers often find waves upset their rhythm, so don't fight it. Just feel the swells and roll with them. A high-elbow recovery is also essential in choppy water. And since you're more buoyant in saltwater than fresh, you can lay off the kick and just focus on your speed-

Your Friends Are Waiting

enhancing front-quadrant swimming and the rhythmic rolling of your hips for power.

4. If it's a triathlon swim, don't sprint at the end. Just hold your pace, keep your heart rate low, and save your energy for the bike and run. As you near shore, swim just until your hands touch bottom, then stand and begin running to shore with a high-knee gait.

— Afterword —
Can Mindful Swimming Enrich Your Life?

My undertaking here is nearly complete. I've written what I hope you'll find to be a practical and encouraging guide to better, smarter swimming, most especially so you might enjoy every lap you ever swim, just as I do. But before I point you to the pool, I'll offer a few final thoughts—not on how to craft a smoother stroke, but to share lessons I've learned from using swimming as an exercise in Mastery and Flow.

In June 2002, I completed the 28.5-mile Manhattan Island Marathon Swim (MIMS). I had two inspirations for this swim. One was turning fifty in 2001 and wanting to undertake a challenge I would never have dreamed of in my twenties. My second inspiration was TI Master Coach Don Walsh, who swam around Manhattan at age fifty and again at fifty-two. When Don set his sights on MIMS the first time, he was advised to prepare by training up to twenty hours—or 60,000 yards—per week for several months. With a job and family, that was out of the question, so he decided to become a more economical swimmer instead and prove he could successfully swim a marathon on a moderate amount of training.

Don took a TI workshop one year before his first Manhattan swim, then tirelessly improved his efficiency through practice, peaking at about 25,000 yards per week. On race day, Don enjoyed his entire nine-hour trip. As he described it, "When the race was over, everyone else was in severe pain. But I felt *great!* If a race official had said, 'Don, you missed a turn and you have to go around again,' I could have done it easily."

Don's secret was matchless efficiency, rather than superhuman fitness. Swimming TI-style, he maintained a leisurely rate of 50 strokes per minute yet kept pace with rivals who were stroking much faster. If you multiply 50 strokes per minute by nine hours, you'll find it took Don 27,000 strokes to swim around Manhattan. If that seems a huge number, consider that everyone else was stroking between 72 and 80 times per minute, taking as many as 41,000 strokes. With the 14,000 strokes Don saved, he could have swum halfway around Manhattan again!

I wanted to train just as Don had—and complete the circuit in fewer strokes! On June 23, 2002, I swam 28.5 miles in a time of 8 hours and 53 minutes, averaging 49 strokes per minute, for a total of just over 26,000 strokes, at least 11,000 fewer strokes than any of my competitors. And like Don, I enjoyed the experience so thoroughly that, within an hour, I had decided to do it again. But the lessons I learned while training for MIMS were just as valuable as the experience of doing it.

In tackling MIMS, I also wanted to demonstrate that one could train for a marathon swim with not a moment of boredom or tedium. For four months, I swam twice as much as I usually do and enjoyed every moment. When other MIMS swimmers learned that I was training solo (I did one session with a friend and three sessions with Masters teams, but more than one hundred hours of training by myself) they commented that I must be going out of my mind having to swim that much by myself. But I enjoyed and was engaged by literally every stroke.

Which is important not just for sanity, but because boredom leads to lack of attention and loss of efficiency. I needed to give *full* attention to each of the approximately 150,000 strokes I took in training, to ensure that each one helped imprint flow and economy as a habit strong enough to survive nine hours of nonstop swimming. My training for MIMS, ultimately, became far less a quest to swim 28-plus miles. It had far more long-term value as an exercise in achieving Mastery and Flow. Let's look at Mastery first.

Anyone Can Be a Master

In 2003, I attended a performance by Geoff Muldaur, a noted blues and roots musician for more than forty years. Sitting just thirty feet away in the small performance space, I was mesmerized by the effortless genius of his guitar playing. He seemed utterly relaxed, almost unconscious, yet his fingers worked the strings with a subtlety I'd never seen to produce sounds of an expressiveness I'd never heard.

Between songs, while telling stories, he never stopped producing beautiful sounds, often with just one hand, all with an amazing casualness. I remarked to my wife, Alice, "I get the feeling we're watching an artist who is never far from his instrument." During a midshow break, while on an outdoor deck, I could see through blinds into the room where he was relaxing . . . which he did by continuing to play as he paced around the room. I knew I was enjoying the privilege of watching a true Master at work.

Afterword

Whenever we witness some form of memorably high-level performance—whether Geoff Muldaur making music or an Olympian in the pool—it's natural to assume that what we're seeing must require some kind of inborn genius. In fact, *anyone* who pursues a personally meaningful challenge—no matter how modest their starting point—can experience the rewards of Mastery.

Mastery is the intriguing process through which something that is initially difficult and frustrating becomes progressively easier and more pleasurable through practice. There may be no better medium than swimming for learning about Mastery because it is the antithesis of a genetically programmed activity. Yet, while human DNA may be poorly wired for swimming, it *is* encoded to learn prodigiously from birth to death.

Mastery in swimming is not about swimming 100 meters in less than a minute nor even solely about achieving stroke efficiency. Like my training for the Manhattan swim, it's about uniting mind and body, without distraction and boredom, in patient, focused, almost loving practice. Practice of this sort can teach you how to perform well in many other ways.

The fundamental creed of the Master is dedication to the value of patience and persistence over the desire for quick and easy results. Cultivate modest expectations along the way and every time you reach a benchmark or breakthrough, enjoy it, then keep practicing, confident you will always have some further plateau to aim for.

Afterword

The Intrinsic Rewards of Practice

An essential insight for mastering any challenging skill is that every brief, but thrilling, spurt forward will be followed by a much longer plateau slightly higher than the previous one. True Masters learn to "love the plateau," continuing to practice enthusiastically even as they seem, on the surface, to be stagnating. While you may mistake those occasional upward surges as the only time progress is occurring, on a deep cellular level, learning and adaptation are constant, whenever you're challenging your body with tasks that require intense concentration.

And true Masters keep practicing primarily *for the rewards of practice itself.* Rather than becoming frustrated by your seeming lack of progress, learn to appreciate your daily routine, just as much as you are thrilled by the occasional breakthrough. Just as Zen practice does, your swimming practice can bring peace and serenity by filling the space usually occupied by the problems and distractions of your external life.

Every time I enter a pool, I enjoy a blissful sense of well-being, because I can *always* do exactly what I want. I may get an electrifying moment of new insight once or twice a year, but the "routine" between those moments is still satisfying because I feel I am never more fully myself than when working on Mastery. The pleasure I have gained from Total Immersion swimming has drawn me to other activities—rowing, yoga, cross-country skiing—that offer similar opportunities for incremental improvement through mindful practice. Together they provide an encouraging sense that, even in my fifties, I'm improving steadily as an athlete.

Afterword

Enriched Experience

The TI way of practicing swimming, as outlined in chapters 6 through 8 and in the sample TI practices (see page 271) is radically different from conventional grind-it-out workouts. TI coaches prefer the term "practice" over "workout" because it implies a very different awareness. For many TI swimmers, the word *practice* is not just something you *do,* but anything you immerse yourself in as an integral part of your life. You practice skilled swimming, not just to swim faster, but for the intrinsic enjoyment it brings.

While some swimmers may exhibit an impatience to move from simple drills to advanced drills to swimming to swimming *fast,* true TI Masters, like Don Walsh, who have been practicing the drills for years, have learned to appreciate the subtleties and endless possibilities contained within even the most rudimentary movements.

On occasion, Don may repeat a single drill—one that he long ago learned to do with what appears to be impeccable form—for thirty minutes or more. Such uninterrupted, meditative repetition expands his awareness significantly. What start out as barely noticeable variations in execution become significant and revealing and can be tweaked with great subtlety. Practice like Don's offers an incredible richness of experience. This newness—new insights, new awareness in "old" skills and movements—banishes boredom and impatience forever.

Afterword

Three Tools for Mastery

As I said earlier, the rewards of Mastery are not reserved only for those gifted with special talents. Practicing like a Master will enable you to achieve a higher level of excellence and a deeper sense of satisfaction. Here are three tools for your journey.

KNOWLEDGE IS POWER

When spending your precious time at practice—and to commit yourself without reservation—it's essential that you be confident you're following the right path. If I have done my job well, this book—confirmed by your body's feedback—can be your source of that certainty. While most of those who read this book are self-coached, a devoted student armed with knowledge is better off than a student with a poor teacher. And even if you have a coach, the ultimate responsibility for success lies not with your teacher but with you.

Videotapes can be a source of guidance and information. If a picture is worth 1,000 words, then a moving picture is probably worth 10,000 words. But learning is immeasurably aided by feedback. And you *can* create feedback for yourself when a teacher isn't available by finding a practice partner.

THE BUDDY SYSTEM

You can work toward Mastery on your own, but it helps to have company on the journey: People who have gone through the same process

Afterword

and can share their wisdom and insight. People who are engaged in the same learning quest as you, with whom you can compare notes. People who are simply interested in your success and will offer encouragement. Best of all is to recruit a practice partner. Share your enthusiasm with them and invite them to join you at the pool. You'll gain a better understanding of what you have been learning if you teach some part of it to a partner . . . and they will then be better prepared to help you right back.

PERFECTION IS NOT THE GOAL

In *Zen in the Art of Archery,* Eugen Herrigel wrote that Zen archers do not train primarily to shoot bull's-eyes, but to increase their self-understanding. Similarly, Mastery is not a pursuit of perfection, but of self-knowledge—including your flaws and limitations. So long as you have human DNA, you'll never reach swimming perfection anyway, so happily you'll always have some greater bliss to aspire to. Further, it's *essential* to feel clumsy or incompetent at times—and to smile at yourself when you do. The understanding of a Master learner is measured by their willingness to surrender what they "know" in order to learn something new.

Making the path to Mastery a powerful habit will enrich the totality of your life experience. Though you began with the limited goal of swimming faster or more efficiently, you can go well beyond that to making swimming a deeply satisfying experience and perhaps to learning life lessons that can enrich nearly any undertaking. For more insights on Mastery, read the book *Mastery: The Keys to Success and Long-Term Fulfillment* by George Leonard.

Afterword

From Fluid Strokes to a Flow State

One Saturday in early November 1970, I had an experience in swimming that mystified me for years after. While swimming in a dual meet for St. John's University, I raced John Quinn, a close friend and rival from Adelphi University, in the 1000-yard freestyle. For several years John and I had swum for Coach Bill Irwin on a club team, Manhasset Swim Club, racing each other day after day in summer training, before heading to our respective colleges in the fall. John was always a bit faster than me in training and held the edge in most of our meet encounters.

On this day, I wasn't especially looking forward to racing him. We were in a hard-training phase and I had felt sore and tired for days. The day before the meet—perhaps because grueling workouts had reduced my resistance—a nasty cold had reached full bloom and I spent the evening dosing myself with orange juice and vitamin C. The morning of the meet I felt sluggish and fuzzy-headed during warmup. Following the 400 medley relay, John and I mounted the center starting blocks for the 1000 free, flanked by two other swimmers from each team. I was aware that this was the most personal rivalry of all the races I would swim during the season.

After the starter's pistol went off, we had swum barely four lengths of that 40-lap race, when I realized that I was swimming as never before. I was slightly in front of the field—I almost always started races behind and then had to catch up—and yet I was swimming with no awareness of effort. Over the next thirty-six lengths, I continued to move effortlessly ahead. I simply felt as if I were floating away from the field—so detached from the race that I almost felt as if I was watch-

Afterword

ing it from the outside. I never felt the slightest pain or fatigue. I never felt as if I was going too hard or too easily. I barely felt as if I was even *doing* it. Yet, despite feeling as if time was suspended, I felt perfectly in control. At the finish, I had lapped everyone in the field, finishing a stunning fifteen seconds faster than the best time I had previously recorded when fully rested and shaved down.

I never matched that time again and I never beat Quinn again. In every subsequent race, he beat me easily. When I sat back down on the team's bench, I just kept shaking my head and saying "I wonder what I could have done if I'd gone *hard?*" What I didn't understand, but realize now, is that I had experienced a rare and elusive experience known as a Flow State—perhaps the richest, most memorable experience any athlete can have, yet one that few ever experience.

Today, I understand Flow well enough to be able to experience it virtually at will, while swimming. And I know that pursuit of Flow, more than the willingness to train hard, is the surest path to swimming your best. When you think about it, what activity could be more perfectly suited to Flow State training than swimming? Everything TI teaches is about achieving more Flow in your stroke. By making Flow State the primary goal, you're simply taking the logical next step.

Bringing Flow to a Conscious Level

Mihaly Csikszentmihalyi, Ph.D., developed the concept of Flow in the 1970s after interviewing artists, or those who were "creating meaning," and he published his groundbreaking insights in the book *Flow: The Psychology of Optimal Experience.* His creative subjects described an ecstatic sense of being outside of what they were creating. Geoff Muldaur might well describe moments of being so fully involved with his music that he barely notices the room or audience, or even his hands or instrument—or at least it appeared that way to me.

Csikszentmihalyi concluded that stepping outside of normal daily routines is an essential ingredient in Flow, as it required an element of creative choice. He also found that most of those who described being in Flow states had seldom analyzed what made them happy. He defined Flow as "feeling completely at one with what you're doing, to know you are strong and able to control your destiny at least for the moment, and to gain a sense of pleasure independent of outcomes." This is exactly the sense I enjoy every time I swim.

The Flow State eludes most athletes and is poorly understood by most coaches. And most of those athletes who *are* fortunate enough to experience Flow do so mainly by chance. But an extraordinary proportion of Total Immersion swimmers, by their own accounts, do experience Flow and—once they have—recreating that state becomes their primary motivation. Swimming faster becomes an almost inevitable result of achieving Flow, rather than the primary goal of their swimming. If Mastery is the purest goal of any Total Immersion swimmer, then knowledge of Flow is the most valuable aid in getting there.

WHAT ARE THE INGREDIENTS OF FLOW?

Csikszentmihalyi described several aspects that are keys to Flow. All have natural links to the program I've laid out in this book:

1. You are involved in an activity that you value and find meaningful. It's safe to say you wouldn't be investing the time to

Afterword

read this book all the way through if you didn't value swimming highly.

2. When involved, you are completely engaged, focused, and concentrating—either because of innate curiosity or because you couldn't succeed if you weren't completely focused. Mindfulness is an organizing principle of TI Swimming and we provide countless aids to, and targets of, focused, attentive swimming.

3. You enjoy great clarity—knowing what needs to be done—and have simple means of monitoring how well it is going. The essential skills of Fishlike Swimming—swimming downhill, *piercing* the water, and moving fluently—provide you with clear goals, while stroke counting and sensory skill practice provide you with ready measures of success.

4. You strike a fine balance between the difficulty of the task and the skills needed to master it. If it were too easy, you'd be bored; if too difficult, you'd grow frustrated. By following the sequence of six progressive lessons in chapter 8, you can easily maintain that fine balance.

5. While involved in your practice, you become so focused on the present task that you enjoy a sense of serenity, of timelessness, and of transcending ego in ways you never have before. Once more, the value of mindfulness that we emphasize as essential to swimming well.

6. You enjoy intrinsic motivation—whatever produces Flow becomes its own reward. And the more rewarding your swimming becomes, the better you become at producing Flow experiences at will, the more you're motivated to practice Total Immersion Swimming—the very definition of a "virtuous cycle."

Afterword

I hope I've given you the tools, insight, and motivation to achieve Mastery and Flow in your own swimming. If so, may you always experience Happy Laps . . . and perhaps one of those laps will one day take you all the way around Manhattan.

Terry Laughlin
New Paltz, New York
November 2002
Terry@totalimmersion.net

Afterword

— Appendix —
Becoming Fit and Fishlike:
Sample Total Immersion Practice Sets

Once you understand that intelligent training is a far more valuable use of your time than mindless lap swimming, you'll ask more penetrating questions about what to do at the pool: How much drill practice, how much sensory skill work, and how much stroke counting will yield the best results? And what's the best way to do them?

Conventional "workouts" mix swim, pull, and kick sets and a few rote drills to get you tired and keep you busy for an hour or so. In TI practice, *every* set has a specific identifiable purpose—and is usually working on more than one level: teaching an essential skill, heightening awareness or imprinting an elusive habit—without neglecting fitness. Every lap is purposeful and mindful.

Here's a starter set of sample practices that show you how to take the lessons of the Total Immersion program and put them into an efficient, effective training format. There are additional suggestions throughout chapter 8 and you can find more sample practices at www.totalimmersion.net. Eventually, as your body learns what being Fishlike should feel like, you'll develop a keen sense of what to concentrate on and how much work you need. In the meantime, these practices will give you some insights toward designing sessions that will keep you tightly focused on improving your economy and making smooth movements a habit while staying fit.

Feel free to modify sets by increasing or decreasing the number of repeats or rounds in a set, or by increasing or reducing the distance of repeats or the suggested rest interval.

Basic Balance Set:
Rest for Three Yoga Breaths Between Lengths

This 500-yard series uses seven balance drills to heighten your awareness of how to achieve a feeling of effortless support in the water—"no more sinking feeling." This helps all your movements gain fluency and economy, and you save energy. Before mixing so many drills in a single set like this, take time to achieve ease and familiarity with each of the individual drills.

> *2 × 25 Balance on Your Back*
> *2 × 25 Head Lead Sweet Spot*
> *2 × 25 Active Balance, see ch. 8, drill 2 (3 yoga breaths each side)*
> *2 × 25 Hand Lead Sweet Spot (25 right side, 25 left)*
> *4 × 25 Skating (alternate 25s right side, left side on next three drills)*
> *4 × 25 UnderSkate*
> *4 × 25 ZipperSkate*

VARIATIONS

- Use as a standard warmup for practices during your first two to six weeks with the TI program.

Appendix: Becoming Fit and Fishlike

- Do the progression two or three times (1000 or 1500 yards) to focus intensively on balance mastery.
- As your balance improves, swim 1 to 2 × 25s or 50s of whole stroke, after each drill, with a focus on feeling just as balanced (supported, relaxed, comfortable) as during the drill.

Drill-Swim Series for Breathing Technique: Rest for Three Yoga Breaths/25 or Five Breaths/50

These balance-and-rotation drills heighten your sense of staying "tall" and balanced while breathing. It also imprints the habit of breathing by "rolling to the air" rather than by turning or lifting the head. Your main focus is staying "tall" and needlelike as you roll to air.

Do 1 to 4 rounds of the following with one length in the drill and one length swim:

2 × 50 or 4 × 25 Skate-Swim
2 × 50 or 4 × 25 UnderSkate-Swim
2 × 50 or 4 × 25 Zipperskate-Swim

In each set of 100 yards, breathe on the left for 50, and the right for 50. When you Skate on your right side (right arm extended), you'll breathe to your left. On the next swim length, breathe to the left side, then switch on the next 50. A second option is to breathe bilaterally (every 3 strokes) on all swim lengths and just focus more on the left side breaths after Skating on your right. On all drill lengths, focus on rolling *past* your Sweet Spot when you roll nose-up to breathe. On all swim lengths, focus on keeping a long, needlelike body position as you roll to the air to breathe.

Drill-Swim Series for "Slippery" Body Positions: Rest for Three to Five Yoga Breaths

This UnderSwitch drill-swim sequence improves your awareness of "piercing" the water while also teaching you to link your arm stroke to the power of core-body rotation.

Do 1 to 4 rounds of ($4 \times 25 + 2 \times 50 + 1 \times 100$) as follows:

4×25: Odd 25s UnderSwitch/Even 25s Swim (try to breathe bilaterally)
2×50: 25 Double UnderSwitch/25 Swim (first 50 left-side breaths, second 50 right-side breaths)
1×100: 25 Triple UnderSwitch/25 Swim (try to breathe bilaterally)

VARIATIONS
- Reverse the order: Do 25s of Triple UnderSwitch/Swim and progress to 100s of UnderSwitch/Swim.
- As your swimming improves, do 25 Drill; 75 Swim on the 100s. "Swim as well as you drill."

Drill-Swim Series to Integrate Drill Skills in Whole Stroke

As your skills improve, increase the proportion of swim-to-drill. The drill lengths heighten balance and alignment; on the swim lengths use focal points that help you take insights gained from the drills into your stroke. Stay committed to the rule of: "Swim as well as you drill."

Swim three rounds of 4 × 100 Drill-Swim as follows:

#1	*25 ZipperSkate/25 Swim (× 2)*
#2	*25 ZipperSwitch/25 Swim (× 2)*
#3	*25 Double ZipperSwitch/Swim 25 (× 2)*
#4	*25 Triple ZipperSwitch/25 Swim (× 2)*
#5–8	*Repeat as above but do 50 Drill/50 Swim*
#9–12	*25 Triple ZipperSwitch/75 Swim*

VARIATIONS:
- Break the 100s into 25s or 50s if you feel any form breakdown.
- Do more sets of 25 Drill/75 Swim as your whole stroke form improves.
- Increase the proportion of multiswitch drills (Double- and Triple Zipper) to develop your rhythm and timing more.
- Substitute Double- and Triple-OverSwitch as a compact, relaxed recovery becomes habit.

Drill-Swim Combinations for Developing Specific Skills or Awareness

The key to transferring drill insights to the whole stroke is to think about doing only one thing really well *on both drill and swim. If you do 25 Skate/25 Swim, and focus on "keeping your head in line" during the drill, then think only about your head position as you swim. Here are some other suggested combinations of drill and focal point for drill and swim:*

DRILL	FOCAL POINT FOR SWIM LENGTHS
UnderSkate	Roll like a needle to breathe; roll all the way to the air.
ZipperSkate	"Lean on your lungs" with light hips and legs; feel supported by the water.
UnderSwitch	Roll freely as you swim.
ZipperSwitch	"Pierce" the water, fitting your body through the smallest possible "hole."
Triple Under	Stay "connected" as you swim; swim with your whole body.
Triple Zipper	Gentle, compact recovery; your hand barely clears the water and reenters immediately.
Triple Over	Cut a hole with your fingertips and slip your arm cleanly through that hole.

VARIATIONS

- Start with multiple lengths of drills, single lengths of swim and progress to fewer drill lengths and more swim lengths.
- Do 200 to 400 yards with one drill and one focal point to imprint it deeply.
- Combine several pairs of drill + focal point in sequence to improve your adaptability.

Take Off the Training Wheels: Whole-Stroke Sets to Develop Stroke Length

These sets teach you how distance affects your stroke efficiency and put you in the habit of critically examining how your training decisions—how far, how hard, how much rest—affect your goals of making efficiency permanent (spl = strokes per length).

STROKE LENGTH EXERCISE 1

Swim 25 + 50 + 75 + 100. Rest for three to five yoga breaths after each swim.

Take note of your stroke count on the 25, then *without trying to strictly limit* your count, just swim at a consistent pace or effort and see what happens to your spl average on the other swims. If you took 15 strokes for the 25, how far above 30-45-60 strokes are you on the 50-75-100? Don't judge yourself; just take note and file the information for future reference.

Sample Total Immersion Practice Sets

STROKE LENGTH EXERCISE 2

Swim 100 + 75 + 50 + 25. Rest for three to five yoga breaths after each swim.

Start with an easy 100. Count your strokes and divide by 4. This number becomes your "N" (benchmark spl) for the rest of the set. Example: If you took 72 strokes, your N is 18 spl (72 divided by 4 lengths). Again, simply note how far below 54-36-18 strokes you are for 75-50-25.

STROKE LENGTH EXERCISE 3

Swim 25 + 50 + 75 + 100.

Repeat Exercise 1, but this time with a specific focal point—e.g., hiding your head, or slipping through a smaller hole, or swimming more quietly. Just take note of your stroke count; don't attempt to hit any particular count. This is purely an experiment to see if technique "tweaks" affect your SL, teaching you that you *can* affect—and ultimately *choose* your SL.

STROKE LENGTH EXERCISE 4

Swim two rounds of 25 + 50 + 75 + 100.

First Round: Swim with fistgloves®. Just swim at your previous effort, not trying to hit any particular count. How many strokes above your ungloved spl are you?

Second Round: Remove fistgloves.® Without *trying* for a particular count, compare your stroke counts to your previous spl to discover how fistgloves® affect your efficiency.

Swimming Golf

We introduce the pace clock, but use spl and perceived effort (heart rate) to measure the "cost" of any speed increases. The easiest way to increase speed isn't more or harder work; it's by learning to swim any given speed more economically, freeing the energy to go farther or faster.

VERSION 1

On successive 50s, swim the same time but reduce your stroke count. Example:

32 total strokes + 50 seconds = a score of 82
31 total strokes + :50 = 81
30 total strokes + :50 = 80

The goal is to repeat the same time on each 50 while continuing to subtract strokes until you can't shave any more from your count without sacrificing speed. Solving it will give you valuable "swimming intelligence."

VERSION 2

On successive 50s, maintain stroke count while descending your time. Example:

30 total strokes + :45 = 75
30 total strokes + :44 = 74
30 total strokes + :43 = 73

Sample Total Immersion Practice Sets

To improve your score you need to keep exactly the same stroke length, but *take each stroke just a bit faster* to shave seconds. You'll be amazed at how quickly a bit more effort can add a lot more strokes. If those strokes don't translate into enough speed to lower your total score, you know you've been wasteful and can take immediate steps to fix the problem.

VARIATIONS ON SWIM GOLF

- "Play" golf with fistgloves®. How close can you come to your ungloved scores? After several rounds with gloves on, do another round without them. Does your score improve over previous ungloved sets after "educating" your hands? If so, lock in the sensations you got.
- How many ways can you score? After you've established your "par," test how many different stroke counts you can swim at a slightly higher score. If your record score is 77, can you swim a constant score of 80 at 30 and 31 and 32 and 33 and 34 strokes? Which feels easiest?
- Take your heart rate or estimate your perceived exertion after a good score. A score of 64 with an HR of 120 is much better than a score of 64 with an HR of 150.

Going Longer: Building Intelligently Toward a Mile Swim

Conventional training for a longer swim is with sheer yardage . . . the main effect of which is to imprint a plodding pace and inefficient stroking. This TI training program imprints an efficient stroke and progressively extends the distances you can maintain that. To prepare for an 800-meter swim, begin with 5 × 100 and increase the number by 1, to reach 10 × 100 in the final week.

1. *Measure your efficiency.* Do a relaxed nonstop swim of 10 to 15 minutes (5 to 10 minutes for a half-mile swim). Count your 25-yard split every 100 or so. If you can you maintain it within 10 percent of your lowest count, you're ready to go longer.

2. *Make Flow and economy a habit.* Don't worry about how far or fast at first; focus on "how right." Swim the benchmark set twice a week. Take eight yoga breaths between repeats. Just count strokes and make Flow and ease a habit. If you lose it, take more yoga breaths and/or slow down.

3. *Build distance but maintain efficiency/economy.* As you increase your benchmark set, keep the focus on ease. Modify only one variable each week. All other variables remain as before.

WEEK 1. Swim 10 × 100. Take six to eight yoga breaths between swims. Maintain spl at least 10 percent lower than on your initial test swim. (For example, if you averaged 20 spl, aim for 18 on your 100s.) Never breathe hard. Finish the set each time feeling as if you could easily keep going like that. If at any time your spl or ease break down, take a recovery break: a 50 of your favorite drill.
WEEK 2. Decrease rest by one breath.
WEEK 3. Increase pace slightly over last 2 × 100.
WEEK 4. Decrease average spl by 1.

Sample Total Immersion Practice Sets

WEEK 5. Increase number of repeats to 12 × 100.

WEEK 6. Decrease rest by one breath.

WEEK 7. Increase pace slightly over last 4 × 100.

WEEK 8. Increase number of repeats to 14 × 100.

WEEK 9. Decrease rest by one breath.

WEEK 10. Increase number of repeats to 16 × 100.

WEEK 11. Increase pace slightly over last 6 × 100.

WEEK 12. Increase number of repeats to 18 × 100.

You don't fail the course if you can't stay precisely with the weekly schedule. Use this as a model for a purposeful, progressive approach to increasing your capacity to maintain an efficient stroke over lengthening distances, imprinting the qualities that produce the *best* long-distance swim, the ability to swim economically for a long time for a duration of your choice.

— Where to Go for What —

Your Directory to Resources
for Better Total Immersion Swimming

Online Help

WWW.TOTALIMMERSION.NET

The Total Immersion Web site will be a priceless source of no-charge support and information. Important features include:

- *Total Swim,* a free newsletter featuring immediately useful articles several times each month. A key ingredient of this newsletter is articles contributed by TI students like you, sharing the insights that have helped them reach their goals. Please consider becoming a contributor.
- An online Discussion Forum for swimmers who are using this book and TI methods to improve their swimming. Use this forum to share your insights, discoveries, and successes, to ask questions and to tap the experience of others who are on the same Mastery path as you.
- Video clips spotlighting key refinements of TI drills and skills.
- Regularly updated samples of TI-specific practices for both technique improvement and effective training.
- A steadily growing directory of trained and certified TI

Coaches available to work with you toward achievement of your goals and complete swimming fulfillment.

- Information on how *you* can become a certified TI Teaching Professional. You may have discovered how difficult it can be to find a qualified instructor who can help you with TI practice. You can be part of the solution. Most of our Teaching Professionals started like you, by learning TI, realizing how simple and effective it is, and wanting to share their discovery with others. Most had never before thought of teaching swimming.

WWW.USMS.ORG

The Web site for U.S. Masters Swimming provides information on joining Masters swimming, links to Local Masters Swim Committees in your area and to Masters Swimming organizations around the world. You can also find a calendar of pool, open-water, and postal swimming events. One of its most helpful features is a directory of thousands of places to swim.

Total Immersion Self-Help Tools

If this book has piqued your interest in developing yourself further as a swimmer, TI offers a growing selection of books and videos/DVDs that distill the complex movements of swimming into simple concepts and progressions that can help *any* swimmer achieve satisfaction and maximize his or her potential. TI books and videos are fully guaranteed to improve your swimming. If at any time you're not satisfied with their quality, contact TI for a full refund *and* you get to keep the book or video. For complete information, visit *www.totalimmersion.net* or call 800-609-7946 or 845-256-9770.

Total Immersion Videos/DVDs

FREESTYLE MADE EASY

Visual reinforcement is priceless in learning physical skills. This 45-minute video illustrates the chapter 8 lesson sequence; each step is examined from above and below water, and in slow motion and stop-action. It also includes special learning refinements from Total Immersion Weekend Workshops to aid "struggling" swimmers, such as the TI Buddy System method, which shows you how to learn faster by collaborating with a friend or partner at any stage of the learning process. Also instruction in freestyle turns, both the relaxing open turn and the fast flip turn. $39.95 VHS or DVD.

HAPPY LAPS: TOTAL IMMERSION FOR BEGINNERS

If you're a nonswimmer . . . if you can swim only a few strokes . . . if you're intimidated by deep water, this is the TI video for you. Illustrates a simple, clear, commonsense approach for learning to be completely at home in the water, experiencing Flow, ease, and real joy—in just a few hours—with a combination of partnered and self-guided "discovery exercises." Lesson One will teach you to be completely comfortable in the water and how to breathe comfortably. Lesson Two teaches you how your body naturally behaves in the water. Lesson Three will teach you to move through the water as fish do, with balanced, *slippery,* whole body movement. $29.95 VHS or DVD.

ALL FOUR STROKES MADE EASY

This DVD illustrates step-by-step skill drills (described in *Swimming Made Easy*) that anyone can master for improved comfort, form, and speed in the four strokes of competitive swimming: butterfly, backstroke, breaststroke, and freestyle. Also includes combo drills that cut learning time in half and help you improve with unprecedented ease and speed. All essential positions and movements illustrated with slow-motion, surface, and underwater views plus advice for the self-coached swimmer with vivid descriptions of how your strokes should *feel* when you're doing them correctly. $29.95 DVD only.

Total Immersion Books

SWIMMING MADE EASY: THE TOTAL IMMERSION WAY FOR ANY SWIMMER TO ACHIEVE FLUENCY, EASE, AND SPEED IN ANY STROKE

If you are encouraged by the development of your freestyle from the guidance in this book, *SME* provides similar guidance on applying the principles of Total Immersion to all four strokes. Refine your form and increase your pleasure with ten lessons, illustrated with 150 surface and underwater photos. Ten chapters on self-coaching show you how to be your own best coach. $19.95.

TRIATHLON SWIMMING MADE EASY: HOW *ANYONE* CAN SUCCEED IN TRIATHLON OR OPEN-WATER SWIMMING

If you think you'd like to venture out from the pool to tackle a triathlon or try your hand at open-water swimming, *TSME* provides a step-by-step learning plan that will help you swim with ease and confidence for *any* distance in *any* body of water. $24.95.

From My Bookshelf

Six well-thumbed titles from my bookshelf have been a priceless source of guidance for me on staying strong and supple at age fifty (or any other age).

Staying Supple: The Bountiful Pleasures of Stretching, by John Jerome (Breakaway Books).

The Supple Body: The New Way to Fitness, Strength, and Flexibility, by Sara Black (Thorsons).

Stretching, by Bob Anderson (Shelter Publications).

Yoga Mind & Body (DK Publishing).

The Pilates Body: The Ultimate At-Home Guide to Strengthening, Lengthening, and Toning Your Body—Without Machines, by Brooke Siler (Broadway).

Pilates on the Ball: The World's Most Popular Workout Using the Exercise Ball, by Colleen Craig (Healing Arts).

Q: Is there a "Total Immersion for Runners"?
A: Yes! *ChiRunning,* by Danny Dreyer.

For years I wished I could find the equivalent for running that has the approach and spirit that Total Immersion brings to swimming. In the fall of 2003, I finally found it. From my teens through my early forties, I had enjoyed running as a reliable source of fitness and the pleasure to be gained from endorphins. I was never a "serious" runner, but I did enjoy participating in the occasional 5K or 10K road race. But from age forty-three to fifty-two I was frustrated by a chronic injury that kept me from running—and triathlons. Whenever I ran farther than about two miles, the soleus muscle (deep tissue at the base of my calf) on my left leg would go into painful spasm. But after reading a pre-release copy of *ChiRunning* (Simon & Schuster), by Danny Dreyer, and attending a one-day ChiRunning workshop (see *www.chirunning.com*) led by Danny, within weeks I was running six miles and more without pain, injury, or fatigue.

Like Total Immersion, ChiRunning takes an activity that many of us do by rote and turns it into an examined activity, developed by mindful practice of intelligent, thoughtful movements. Like Total Immersion, the emphasis is on improving your speed and endurance through more effective movement, rather than more and harder miles. And best of all, like Total Immersion, it works! So if you have been encouraged by how Total Immersion has affected your swimming, and you'd like to have a similar experience with running, I recommend you check out ChiRunning.

— Index —

Index

Index

Index

Index

Index